FLORENC NIGHTINGALE
A LIFE INSPIRED

Born to Privilege

Florence Nightingale was born with a dilemma: She was born and raised in the Unitarian Church, which regards good works as the acid test of religious conviction, but she was also born and raised to be a decorously idle Victorian lady.

Nightingale was a devout Christian all her life, and her writings and actions demonstrated both the published beliefs of the Unitarian Church and its unspoken assumptions. As a Unitarian, Nightingale believed that theology was less important than was action to redress injustice and to uplift the poor and suffering. Unitarianism tells its congregants to let others worry about theology and instead to get out there and do something to help the community. Like most Unitarians, Nightingale valued independent thought and privately considered it a form of arrogance to attempt a full human understanding of God's nature and wishes.

Victorian social mores, however, were in direct contradiction to that message. Many historians of the nineteenth century have noted the stark contrasts in lifestyle between the leisure and working classes. In the working classes, women were fully expected to work side by side with their husbands and fathers in farming, keeping house, minding a shop, or serving a wealthy family.

But Florence Nightingale was not born into such a family. She was, instead, born to a wealthy English couple who could afford a honeymoon that took several years and spanned the European continent. The honeymoon of William Edward and Frances Nightingale went on for so long that their two daughters were both born before the couple returned to their home in England. Florence was named after the Italian city where she was born. Her sister, Frances Parthenope, was similarly named in honor of her parents' travels: Parthenopolis is an ancient Greek settlement in Naples.

Florence's father inherited his fabulous wealth and his aristocratic title from his great-uncle, Peter Nightingale. Nightingale had made a fortune in lead mining, and when he died, that fortune and the noble arms and name of the Nightingale clan fell to William Shore, who became William Edward Nightingale, often referred to affectionately as WEN.

His great work was the meticulous care and education of his two daughters. Despite his extensive efforts to educate his children far beyond what was typical for young English ladies of the time, his eldest daughter, Parthenope, took after her mother and cared more for parties and dresses than for books or ideas. Florence, however, took after her father, and the time he spent teaching her history, philosophy, and a multitude of languages, both modern and ancient, was not wasted. Therefore, while other well-born young English women were learning to dance, paint in watercolors, and play adeptly at the piano, Florence was learning Greek, Latin, and the history of the British constitution.

Nightingale was clearly not cut out for a life of dances, teas, and gossip. At the age of seventeen, she experienced a profound religious calling. It happened at the family estate of Embley, where two giant cedar trees had formed an outdoor sanctuary for meditation. Her call from God was fairly specific. It did not ask her to adopt a life of meditation. Rather, in her writings, Nightingale said that God had assigned her a "quest." What that quest was, she did not then know. History suggests, however, that her quest was to improve medical care for the ages by elevating the status of nurses and calling for better hospital construction and sanitation.

In 1835 Nightingale's father formed a plan to take his family on another tour of continental Europe. That plan finally came to fruition two years later. The trip accomplished two things: It would provide an unrivalled educational opportunity for his daughters. It also provided an opportunity to convert his relatively modest Georgian manor into a mansion that would suit the social ambitions of his wife. Florence herself had a further hope—that this trip would provide some insight into the meaning of God's call.

The Nightingales took the educational dimension of travel seriously and packed accordingly. Their correspondence shows that a great deal of consideration went into choosing a travel library that would support their overseas learning. Guides to the identification of plants and animals were considered, as were the works of John Milton and William Shakespeare.

The Nightingales' travel itinerary was fairly predictable. They arrived in France, debarking from a ship called *The Monarch*, and then traveled by a private carriage that was large enough to accommodate two parents, two daughters, a nanny, and a maid. They hit all the major sightseeing destinations in France, such as Chartres, the Loire River valley, Biarritz, Avignon, and the Riviera. Around Christmas-time, they settled down in Nice for several weeks.

Both Frances and William Edward Nightingale were socially well-connected. Everywhere the family went, they met with people of social or political influence. As a result, Florence was able to learn not just from an observation of cathedrals, museums, and monuments, but also from conversation with many leaders of thought and culture.

Florence kept detailed journals of what she was learning, and it is clear that she was not only interested in humanity's great artistic achievements, like the Chartres cathedral; she was also interested in humanity's signal failures. She often took detours from the approved tourist path to visit hospitals, prisons, and charitable institutions. Her eyes would wander from the spires of a great basilica to the beggars in the square below. Everywhere she went, she was sensitive to the great beauty of European architecture, but she could not help also noticing the poor and sick.

She noted the multiple war wounds of the Blaye Cathedral caretaker who took them on a tour of the church. He had fought in and been wounded in the Napoleonic wars. Florence could not help but notice many such men who were permanently disabled from serving in the military. She found herself fascinated with nineteenth-century France's welfare laws.

From Nice, the Nightingales proceeded to Italy. They stayed a month in Genoa. The family's lives were a whirl of balls, opera, and social engagements, but in her letters, Florence seems to have been more interested in a group home for the deaf and dumb that she visited. She was struck by an inner light in the inhabitants, yet she was appalled by their care. In her notes, she described them as sick and "melancholy." The home did not meet her standards of cleanliness.

After their stay in Genoa, the Nightingales made their way to Florence. There, as elsewhere, the family attended the opera. Florence's letters home betray that she was frequently seduced by this form of entertainment. Italian opera was gorgeous in a way that made English opera seem like a poor cousin. The family stayed in Florence long enough for Florence to take music lessons, specializing in singing and piano, while her sister studied drawing.

Florence was drawn to the arts, but she was equally dazzled by the ideas of Giuseppe Mazzini, an advocate for the working class and for Italian independence. She identified with Mazzini's beliefs, and she observed for herself that the Italian nobility lived in far too much luxury, oblivious of the extreme poverty of the nation's have-nots. She wrote scathingly about a Holy Week tradition that required the Grand Duchess to wash and kiss the feet of the city's poor. Clearly, the intention of the ceremony was to obliterate class distinctions. Yet the duchess, Nightingale observed, had interpreted this ritual to mean that she washed only a small spot on each foot. This was the spot that she then kissed while chaperoned by her chamberlain and her lady-in-waiting, who flanked her, one on each side.

On their way to Switzerland, the Nightingales stopped in Bologna and Venice. When they arrived in the Geneva lake district, they were welcomed by a number of delighted acquaintances, many of whom remembered William Edward from his previous tour twenty-two years earlier.

It was through this network of acquaintances that Florence met and fell partly under the spell of Jean Charles Leonard Sismondi, a writer and historian. Sismondi was critical of the industrial revolution because of the way it polarized factory owners and workers into two classes defined, on one side, by excessive wealth and, on the other side, by abject poverty. Sismondi's formalized ideas resonated with Florence's observations about poverty in Europe and the sharp divisions between rich and poor.

The Nightingales' Swiss tour was cut short when Louis Bonaparte Napoleon, nephew to the notorious former French dictator, entered Switzerland with French military troops hot on his trail. The family didn't flee, precisely, but they travelled non-stop for several days, finally reaching Paris around the same time of Napoleon's rendition to England.

In Paris, Florence had the great good fortune to spend time in the salon of Mary Clarke, an English expatriate living in Paris. At that time, French salons were where the most famous and influential artists, writers, and thinkers met to socialize and discuss ideas. Though Clarke was a year older than Florence's father, Mary and Florence became fast and lifetime friends. Through her friendship with Mary, Florence met novelist Victor Hugo, poet Madame Tastu, and French political historian Alexis de Tocqueville.

But the friendship with Clarke herself was more influential on Florence's future self than were any of the more stellar celebrities whom Florence met at Clarke's home. In Clarke, Florence finally encountered a woman who defied most of Victorian tradition. She was a prolific writer, formerly a portrait artist, and an advocate for women's rights. She wore what she wanted, without deference to nineteenth-century propriety. She lived independently and surrounded herself with male intellectuals, dismissing women from her company unless, like Florence, they distinguished themselves in some way. It would be a mistake to underestimate the importance of Clarke as a role model for Florence's future decisions. Clarke showed, if no one else did, the possibilities that lay before a Victorian lady if she had the courage to defy social norms and carve her own destiny.

After roughly two years of travel, the Nightingales returned to England, stopping at London for the social season. It was, in Frances Nightingale's mind, a pivotal moment in her daughter Florence's life. Florence was now almost nineteen years old, and it was time to "present her to society." For girls born to Florence Nightingale's station, an important rite of passage marking the transition from child to woman was a formal presentation to the queen.

Florence was duly presented to Queen Victoria in the latter's drawing room on a May day in 1839. As was the custom, she approached the young queen when her name was called, curtsied, kissed Victoria's hand, and then exited the room, walking backward so as not to turn her back on the monarch. There was only one year's age difference between the two young women; Victoria was barely Florence's senior. Florence had bought a white dress for the occasion, and in her writings, she wryly notes that the queen looked tired. It was the first, but not the last, meeting between these two titans of history.

There can be no doubt that, in presenting her daughter to the queen and giving her a London season, Frances Nightingale fully expected her daughter to strike the fancy of an eligible young bachelor. Florence's trajectory would then be marriage, a proper English manor well-equipped with servants, and eventually, children. In this, Frances was to be deeply disappointed. She appears to have been willfully blind to the many signs that Florence had no real aptitude for the life of a conventional Victorian lady.

The novelty of the summer social season quickly dimmed for Florence. She met many young and beautiful people in her London summer, but the person who seems to have had the most impact on her was the famed mathematician Charles Babbage, who is sometimes credited with inventing technology leading to the computer. Florence met up with her new friend Mary Clarke and confided in the latter that she found a comforting sense of certainty in mathematics.

By the time she was twenty, her father may have realized to his regret that, through his efforts to educate Florence, he had created not a monster but, to be sure, a young woman who could never be content within the confines of a conventional Victorian life. In 1840, a typical twenty-year-old woman from a family as well off as the Nightingales would either be engaged, or it would be her life's work to become engaged. Once married, she would give birth to a few children, take an occasional interest in their care, and socialize intensively with other wealthy people in her community. England of 1840 expected its young, affluent women to be literate and culturally astute, but it provided no real occupation for women with energy and vision. Fields of endeavor that were open to energetic, ambitious men—the military, finance, law, medicine, manufacture—were effectively closed to women.

So when Florence Nightingale came of age, there was no obvious pathway for a woman who wished to take charge and live a life of action. Even her modest request—to study mathematics—was a controversial move and one that her father had to consider carefully before giving his consent. She undertook these studies under the direction of a private tutor and, with her characteristic seriousness, applied herself to the field with rigor.

But her study of mathematics did not lead to the life of action and heroism for which Florence Nightingale yearned, and what followed was a decade of mostly thwarted ambition and longing. During these fallow years, she wrote an essay titled "Cassandra" that bemoaned the position of young women in England. "Cassandra" finds young women of Nightingale's age singing Schubert and embroidering, activities she clearly finds trivial. Meanwhile, she berates the lack of passion in women's lives, which she sees as artificially instilled by a repressive upbringing.

We don't know exactly when Florence became interested in the nursing profession. She did frequently take an interest in the health of ailing relatives. Throughout her twenties, she sat at the bedsides of sick villagers and did what she could, with no training, to ease their suffering. She was also generous with money. However, she always felt stifled in her ambition to do more. She complained about the obvious differences between her status as a wealthy do-gooder and the status of the poorest people whom she meant to benefit. Without embedding herself in a community of sufferers, she would always be a sort of well-meaning tourist. In her writings, she sagely noted that pulling up to a poor person's house in an expensive carriage and dropping off money is hardly a life modeled on that of Jesus Christ.

Florence got an opportunity to observe hospitals and nurses through a family friend, Elizabeth Herbert. Herbert and her husband also enjoyed great wealth, and they had turned much of their philanthropic attention to hospital conditions and reform.

When she was twenty-four, Florence indicated her interest in the nursing profession, but her parents were strongly opposed. It needs to be noted that, in the nineteenth century, nurses did not enjoy the reputation that they enjoy today. In fact, the reputation they enjoy today is largely due to the reforms brought about by Florence Nightingale. Nineteenth-century nurses fell into two categories: There were nursing nuns, who achieved a modicum of the respect due to their hard work and lives of strict sacrifice. Lay nurses, however, were another story. They were widely assumed to be alcoholics and victims, if not willing participants, of sexual harassment from patients and other medical professionals. Outside the church, nursing was the last refuge of a woman who could find no other way to earn her living. It was not, in brief, the career path that a young lady brought up in a wealthy Victorian home would consider— unless that young lady were Florence Nightingale.

Nightingale was so bent on becoming a nurse that she attempted to convert to Catholicism. To that end, she met with Cardinal Manning and posed the question of whether, as a Catholic, she might be better positioned for a life of service. Manning deflected her petition. Officially, he discouraged Florence's conversion because her theology was not aligned with Catholic belief, even though she was quite spiritual. It's likely, though, that he also believed she would be using the Catholic infrastructure to obtain the nurse training and career of which she dreamed.

Florence Nightingale's decision to be a "spinster" was not the work of a moment but, rather, an idea framework that evolved over a period of nine years, during which she was unsuccessfully wooed by Richard Monckton Milnes. Milnes was a baron and a writer whose most important work, *Life, Letters, and Literary Remains of John Keats*, established the poet John Keats in the pantheon of Romantic poets. Milnes was eleven years older than Florence. They met in 1842, when Florence was twenty-two and he was thirty-three. Milnes was a philanthropist, and he shared Florence's zeal for reform. He deserves praise for insisting that prisons separate children from the general adult population of criminals. This action paved the way for reform schools, which, if they are not always successful in their mission, are still an improvement on throwing a twelve-year-old into the same cell as a thirty-year old murderer.

Like Clarke, Milnes was famous for hosting a sort of English salon. Only, his gatherings took place over breakfasts, to which he invited notable scholars, politicians, and other luminaries. The social commentator Thomas Carlyle once quipped that if

Christ were to return to earth, Richard Monckton Milnes would get a jump on everyone else and invite him to breakfast.

But Florence continued to dream of being a nurse. She helped the sick in West Wellow Village, a small community near the family's Embley estate. There she experienced frustration when she saw what poor care the sick sometimes received. At one point, she witnessed the slow death of a woman in the village. In a letter to her cousin, Florence hinted that the poor woman's illness was treatable, but the "fools" who were attending her were far too ignorant to help her. Florence even suggested that the woman was poisoned by those who were supposed to be administering her care.

She continued to act as an unacknowledged and unpaid nurse wherever the opportunity presented itself. In 1843 her friend Harriet Martineau fell ill, and Nightingale rushed to her bedside to offer care. Martineau was already a famous writer, specializing in political and social science. She and Nightingale shared an interest in the plight of the poor and in social reform. Nightingale had met Martineau during her "coming out" season in London, and the two had stayed in touch since. In her letters, Martineau described herself as one of Nightingale's first patients. When she ran to Martineau's bedside, little did Nightingale know that she was banking credit for her fight for army reform. Martineau would, in the near future, prove an invaluable ally in that endeavor.

Then, in 1845, an opportunity for medical training seemed to fall into her lap. Dr. Richard Fowler, a family friend, offered her the opportunity to train as a nurse at Salisbury Hospital for three months. At twenty-five, Florence was more than ready to enter the working world. But her mother reacted quickly and vehemently to squelch that plan. Frances declared nursing an unladylike profession far beneath Florence's place in society. Frances feared that Florence would be propositioned by unsavory men, but, above all else, she worried what people would think. She failed to understand how Florence could even propose such a course of action. Fowler's own wife joined her voice to that of Frances. The hospital was far too coarse a place for a young woman like Florence, Mrs. Fowler opined. Florence reluctantly bowed to her mother's will, but in a bitter letter, she wrote that she had no real reason to continue living and that her only real achievement to date was becoming less and less ladylike with every passing year. She wrote that she felt crushed by a life of vanity and deceit and that she felt herself to have less value than dust.

As he approached the age of forty, Florence's suitor, Milnes, became anxious to have things settled between himself and the object of his affection. In considering Milnes' petition for her hand in marriage, Florence was torn. Certainly, her family would be relieved if she married, and here was a man who was more than eligible. She acknowledged that he was her intellectual equal and that he was a passionate person, as she was.

To say that Milnes was a patient man would be something of an understatement. Elizabeth Gaskell, a historian of that time, described him as "at the feet" of Florence Nightingale for nine years. When he became her suitor, they exchanged letters, quipped about favorite writers, and visited at least one museum together. But Nightingale was terrified of a gilded cage. Marriage to Milnes, she imagined, could turn into a schedule of society functions, dancing, tea, and chit-chat. Horrors! She finally gave him a definitive "no" in 1849 at a Whitsun party hosted by the Nightingales at their Embley estate. He took his marching orders to heart, marrying a young woman named Annabel Crew shortly thereafter.

There is considerable evidence that Florence was anguished by their split. She would, naturally enough, have been full of self-doubt and second-guessing. The two of them had quite a bit in common, and he had offered her genuine friendship and a partnership of equal minds. It is a testament to both Florence and Milnes that they remained friends for the rest of their lives, despite the mutual disappointment that they both felt at the end of their romantic attachment.

Kaiserswerth

It's difficult to say at what point Florence managed to change her family's mind about allowing her to live independently and pursue a career. Certainly, her definitive refusal of Milnes demonstrated that she would not be gently bullied into compliance. A second call from God further catalyzed Florence, and this time she felt that God was telling her, perhaps not to defy her parents, but that his plan for her was more important than theirs.

Florence finally got the training in nursing and hospital management that she had longed for, albeit in a very roundabout way. To console her for the loss of Milnes, family friends Charles and Selina Bracebridge took her on a tour of Egypt, Greece, and central Europe. It was in Egypt, near the banks of the Nile River, that Nightingale heard her second call from God. And this time, she heard a voice that asked her whether she could really hesitate in choosing the will of God over her "little reputation." This may have been the breakthrough moment for Nightingale. She herself, of course, had never worried about her reputation, but her family had asked her to put it first. Now a call from God had clarified that reputation was not a priority. It would be a mistake to underestimate the importance of this moment in Nightingale's ability to break free at last from her family's protection.

In 1850, while traveling in Germany with the Bracebridges, Nightingale got the opportunity to visit the Deaconess's Institute of Kaiserswerth, a charitable hospital mostly run by Protestant deaconesses, who were effectively nurses. The hospital's 116 deaconesses, sixty-seven of whom had received actual nurse training, served one hundred patients. Nightingale visited the hospital as a live-in guest for two weeks, and the Bracebridges conspired with her to keep this visit a secret from her parents and sister.

The Kaiserswerth Institute was a revelation for Nightingale. Here was a collection of hardworking and respectable nurses who were not bound to the church with unbreakable oaths. They defied the polarization of nineteenth-century nurses, who were usually either virtuous Catholic nuns or desperate women of low repute. While the position of "deaconess" is a religious one, deaconesses, like Protestant deacons, are not ordained and therefore have no lifelong tie to celibacy or communal living. There can be no question that the deaconesses of Kaiserswerth provided a model of nursing that was both respectable and almost secular.

Nightingale was fascinated by the Kaiserswerth hospital, and she wrote a thirty-two page booklet that reported her observations of the institute. The booklet, titled *The Institution of Kaiserswerth on the Rhine for the Practical Training of Deaconesses under the Direction of the Rev. Pastor Fliedner, Embracing the Support and Care of a Hospital, Infant and Industrial Schools*, did a lot more, however, than just report on the success of the German hospital. In it, Nightingale explored the origins of nursing in early Christianity. The apostle Paul referred to women deacons in letters that have become part of the New Testament. Using these references as evidence, Nightingale argued in her book that women had been called to serve God as nurses since the Pauline age.

In Nightingale's mind, it was significant that these early deaconesses, as well as the ones working at Kaiserswerth, did not take vows or live in cloisters. As such, they almost provided an example of church/state separation. Nightingale had started to believe that, to be successful, nursing would need to be separate from the church, even though she believed that nursing was a spiritual calling.

The Nightingales back home had learned of Florence's "secret" visit to Kaiserswerth, and they reacted with fear and anger.

Parthe, in particular, was so anxious that she became ill. Florence returned to the bosom of this family, but she did not thrive. Her journals show that, while she was not suicidal, she had a death wish. She believed she was starving—not for food, which was plentiful in her family, but for meaningful work. She was never hungry for intellectual stimulation. Great leaders and thinkers were constantly visiting the Nightingale estate. By this time in her life, however, Florence felt frustrated by intellectual chat. She wanted to put ideas into action. She yearned to do, not just to think and talk.

Her writings from this time show that she was deeply critical of her family. She condemned her father, William Edward, as a mostly idle man who had not found an appropriate outlet for his talent and energy. He would, she thought, have been in his element running a factory and managing a staff of three hundred, but his wealth had effectively cut him off from that avenue. Nightingale was far ahead of her time in noting that wealth can be a disincentive. Her father's problem was that money had freed him from struggle, and struggle is what makes life interesting. Florence's analysis of her mother and sister was equally damning. She found her mother trivial, over-invested in her social circle, and blissfully unaware that she was missing something. Similarly, Parthe's drawing room-centric life fit her like a glove, and she failed to imagine anything better.

In 1851, Florence had the good fortune to meet another woman who inspired her as Mary Clarke had done. Dr. Elizabeth Blackwell, the first woman medical doctor in the United States, was finishing her medical training in London when she met Nightingale at the home of Sidney and Elizabeth Herbert. Blackwell was a year younger than Florence, and she provided the latter with more evidence that a life of deprivation can thrust one into greatness, whereas wealth and privilege allow one to idle.

Blackwell had been born into a comfortable middle-class home. Her father was a successful businessman specializing in the refinement of sugar. However, by the time Blackwell was seventeen, her family's fortunes had declined. A fire that destroyed their refinery and other troubles caused them a considerable loss of income and luxury. Then her father died, leaving the family in debt. Elizabeth Blackwell went into teaching and eventually landed a job that paid $400 a year. Out of that modest salary, she saved enough money to pay for medical school.

Florence Nightingale had been forming the theory that adversity makes people persistent and imaginative, and here was living proof. Blackwell had been refused admission from several medical schools before she succeeded in her goal, yet here she was, about to become a doctor. Furthermore, she had a kind of war wound: Blackwell had been routinely treating a child for eye disease when some of the solution shot into her own eye. An infection ensued, and she lost that eye. Her glass replacement did not dim her energy or enthusiasm for her upcoming medical career, however. Clearly, she and Nightingale had a great deal to talk about.

Blackwell tried to talk Florence's family into allowing her to train in medicine. But Blackwell's own history—the loss of an eye, the gracelessness of a glass replacement—horrified the Nightingales. In Blackwell, they saw their fears for Florence confirmed. Nevertheless, Florence had met a woman who lived life on her own terms, and that lesson could not and would not be unlearned.

Some dynamic between Florence and her family had altered. In her writings, she no longer worried about their approval. Instead, she wrote that she must quit seeking their help and sympathy and put their relationship on a "true footing." Her parents may have sensed this sea change, because they agreed to let Florence return to Germany for a three-month stay at the Kaiserswerth Institute. It was a sort of internship, and it was the only real training that Florence would receive prior to the wartime career that made her famous.

She threw herself into this apprenticeship with tireless vigor. At thirty-two, she was older than most of the deaconesses, who were mostly in their twenties, but she joined them in wearing the standard-issue, blue-print hospital dress. For the first time in her life, she had to groom herself with no servant's assistance and do her own hair. It was exactly the opportunity she had longed for—to live as an equal in a community of medical professionals, not just as a lady bountiful visitor.

Nightingale wrote prolifically about what she observed at Kaiserswerth. She learned a great deal, but she could also see the need for change. She sat at the bedside of a man who died in agony following the amputation of a leg. For several days, she read to him and applied wet compresses to his stump. While the use of chloroform made him more comfortable during the operation itself, Florence's notes suggest that she had some questions for the attending doctor. He did not, she noted in her journal, cut away the dead and rotting skin around the amputation.

Following the practice of the day, Nightingale and another nurse applied leeches to the patient's forehead when he developed a fever. Medical science at that time believed that the loss of blood could benefit a patient. Today, we know that the opposite is true, but "bleeding" was still a common practice in Nightingale's time. It is not entirely clear at what point Nightingale decided that bleeding did more harm than good. We do know that she discouraged it when she arrived in the Crimea. It is therefore likely that she began to reject the theory of bleeding at Kaiserswerth, where her amputee patient died of complications after a sordid struggle of several days. In her notes, Nightingale also observed that the patient's sisters were not allowed to see his body and that it broke their hearts.

Upon her return to England, Nightingale had an opportunity to put some of her nurse's training into action. Her own father had fallen ill. He suffered from a recurring eye infection and constipation. Florence accompanied him to the Umberslade spa near Birmingham for a "water cure." Water cures were not that different from today's spa treatments. Patients, usually wealthy people who could afford to travel and stay in attractive lodgings, were presumed to benefit from hot baths, cold showers, good food, and exercise.

WEN did, in fact, improve under this regime. He went on long walks and ate nourishing meals. The spa doctor made him quit taking quinine, a medication that has some possible applications for malaria patients but is not indicated for anyone else and can lead to paralysis and death. Under further advice from his doctor, WEN ate more whole grain bread and vegetables. We know now that dietary fiber and exercise do contribute to good health. While nineteenth-century medicine was still in the dark about a lot of matters, the regime at Umberslade was truly therapeutic, mostly because it encouraged exercise and nutrition without attempting invasive procedures. At the Umberslade spa, Florence had a chance to see the benefit of good nutrition, bathing, and a hygienic environment. It was also obvious that the rich patients at Umberslade, with their minor ailments, were getting better care than the poor amputees at Kaiserswerth.

Independence

It was not until she was thirty-two that Nightingale finally got her break. She was hired to superintend a sort of nursing home for retired governesses called the Care of Sick Gentlewomen in Upper Harley Street. "Hired" is something of a euphemism because it was actually a volunteer position. Nightingale received no salary and had to support herself with a small allowance of five hundred pounds a year that her father bestowed on her. To modern ears, it sounds like an appallingly small sum, but in Victorian England, it was in fact a sufficiency. Armed with that allowance, Nightingale finally achieved her dream of leaving home and renting a small apartment in the Pall Mall district. She retained the services of a housekeeper, who doubled as a chaperone.

In her new position, Nightingale immediately demonstrated the leadership potential that would make her famous in the upcoming Crimean War. The patients had yet to arrive when she took charge, making improvements in the infrastructure. She wasted no time in making the institution work more efficiently. She demanded the installation of a dumbwaiter to carry medical supplies and food to the various floors of the home. She also implemented a system of bells that allowed the nursing staff to know which patient needed attention.

Nightingale's supervision extended beyond making the home efficient. Operated on private donations, the Harley Street home was, initially, designed exclusively for Protestant patients. The home's directors intended to decline applications from Catholic women. Nightingale put her foot down immediately and declared that the home would accept women of all religions or she would resign. Her ultimatum carried the day, and the home became ecumenical in its outreach.

The Harley Street clientele was a collection of sad women, indeed. They were governesses who were either very sick or out of work. Most of them were unwanted by their families. It is worth noting that, in Victorian England, governesses were almost invariably well-born young ladies whose families had fallen on hard times. They worked long hours for wealthy families, often put up with abusive children, and made a pittance. It was rare for a governess to save any significant amount of money. The Harley Street home was a way station for some and an end-of-life hospice for others.

Nightingale was shocked at the slatternly conditions of the Harley Street home. Frayed carpets and bare windows were bad enough, but it also happened that the mattresses, blankets, and pillows were so nasty that some of them were positively rotting.

Rats and mice owned the place. Nightingale swung into action, got the house cleaned up, and marshaled her own housekeeper and two other women to sew new pillowcases, towels, tablecloths, and dish clothes. Ragged materials were all repurposed. Old curtains were refashioned into seat covers, and new rugs were patched together out of intact fragments.

Nightingale then turned her attention to the food supply. Food for patients was delivered several times a day, and she was dismayed to learn that biscuits and jam were being purchased ready-made. She insisted that food be ordered in bulk and that the staff make its own jam and biscuits. This economy not only improved the efficiency of the institution; it also saved money. Nurses who did not meet the high new bar were summarily dismissed. In her journals, Nightingale reports dismissing one nurse for opium addiction and another for being dirty.

The governesses rightly adored Nightingale. She worked tirelessly on their behalf and literally saved several of their lives. When an ether prescription came mislabeled from the pharmacy, she caught the mistake before her patients drank it. One of her patients required a mastectomy, and Nightingale's postoperative care prevented infection. Delivered from breast cancer, that governess was able to return to work.

Nightingale was worried, however, that some of her "patients" were not truly sick. At that time, "hysteria" was a convenient, catch-all, and completely bogus diagnosis for women who did not fit in well with their environments, for whatever reason. Many such "hysterics" found their way to the Harley Street facility. Some of them, Florence thought, just needed to quit being idle and find something useful to do with themselves. She tactfully provided them with letters of recommendation and even small sums of money, taken directly out of her own pocket, but she warned the home's supervisory board that the facility could easily turn into a safe harbor for the idle if patients were not more carefully screened.

In brief, she needed more of a challenge than the Harley Street project provided. And she did not have to wait long for such a challenge to present itself: a cholera epidemic in London beckoned. The epidemic targeted the neighborhood of Broad and Oxford Streets near Soho Square. Consequently, Nightingale volunteered her services at the nearby Middlesex Hospital.

Cholera was and is a deadly disease that kills its victims, sometimes within hours of their first symptom. At the Middlesex Hospital, Nightingale witnessed the extremes of dehydration first hand. The epidemic hit the neighborhood's prostitutes particularly hard. Some of her patients were literally husks of their former selves. Nightingale had, as a volunteer, walked into a deadly environment where many of the paid staff had walked off their jobs for fear of their lives. There were no known treatments for the disease, and doctors of the time had only the vaguest idea that cholera's transmission was through the water supply.

Nightingale worked tirelessly with her patients without contracting the disease. She sat at the death-beds of two nurses who were not so lucky and contracted cholera. Having run the gauntlet unharmed, she came to believe, erroneously of course, that she enjoyed some kind of special immunity to cholera. The truth is that her meticulous attention to hygiene saved her. No doubt, she kept scrupulously clean and avoided sharing any water or drinking vessels with the patients and hospital staff.

Crimea

The British involvement in the Crimean War was a disaster from start to finish. Ships bearing food and supplies for soldiers went off course or delivered to the wrong port. Supplies went mysteriously "missing" on a regular basis. Meanwhile, politicians quibbled in the houses of parliament about whether the government or the soldiers themselves were responsible for providing their own fuel. According to terms of service that enlisted men signed, they were officially responsible for providing their own fuel, a line of fine print that didn't stop them from freezing to death in tents and trenches when blanket and clothing deliveries failed.

Across all armies sent to the Crimean War, the death rate was twenty percent, and infection killed many more soldiers than did their enemies. To put that into context, the mortality rate of U.S. soldiers in the Vietnam War was 2.6 percent. The Crimean War took place twenty years before the germ theory was unveiled. Without the germ theory, the spread of infection was an unsolved medical mystery. Arguably, Florence Nightingale's greatest achievement was her ability to link infection to unclean environs despite the absence of the germ theory. Nightingale's patients were also around a hundred years too early to benefit from the advent of antibiotics.

The Turkish Selimiye Barracks in Scutari had been haphazardly retrofitted as a hospital for British soldiers fighting in the Crimean War. Located within what we know today as the Turkish city of Istanbul, the Barracks Hospital was a perfect storm of inexperience, incompetence, and criminal negligence. It was overcrowded. Beds were crammed within eighteen inches of each other. It was filthy. Supplies like bandages and medications were virtually non-existent. There wasn't even enough food to feed the patients properly. There was a similar lack of clothing and blankets. It was not unusual for a soldier on his death-bed to be fully naked.

There was no kitchen or laundry room. Running underneath the facility was a sewer crawling with rats. In a letter home, Nightingale quipped that the only thing preventing the rats from stealing all the hospital beds was their inability to organize. There was no central gas lighting. Instead, rooms and procedures were lit by candles, often hastily shoved into beer bottles that served as impromptu candle-holders. It comes as no surprise that the death rate was appallingly high.

Infection, typhus, typhoid, and dysentery picked wounded soldiers off like flies, and sixty percent of the patients admitted with cholera died. Soldiers who were sent to the hospital with non-fatal conditions ended up dying from pneumonia or dysentery contracted from other patients. Infections did not need to be airborne to kill because the soldiers were crawling with lice, the champion vectors of disease transmission. But the truly staggering death toll took place amongst the amputees. At the Barracks Hospital in Scutari, eighty-two percent of patients who underwent an amputation died in postoperative care. Soldiers who were hastily butchered by field doctors stood a statistically much better chance of survival—a testament to the unhygienic conditions at the hospital.

The hospital in Scutari was not uniquely bad amongst military hospitals of the time. It was unique only in that it had attracted the attention of the *London Times*, which reported its horrific conditions faithfully to the public and caused a terrible public relations scandal for those politicians in charge of the war effort. The public outrage threatened to topple the government, especially when it came out that the French were doing a marginally better job of caring for their wounded. The Crimean War earned the distinction of being the first time in British history that a medical corps was accused of negligence.

Into this fray, a thirty-four-year-old Florence Nightingale was sent with a meager year of hospital experience under her belt.

By today's standards, her appointment to the hospital in Scutari was flagrantly nepotistic. Her old family friend, Sir Sidney Herbert, who served at that time as the British Secretary of War, declared that Nightingale was the only person in the realm who could succeed at the Barracks Hospital. Nepotism or not, it was not immediately clear that Herbert did Nightingale any favors with this appointment. Cleaning up that hospital and bringing some sense of order was a Herculean task.

Nightingale arrived in Turkey in November of 1854 with thirty-eight nurses, one of them her beloved Aunt Mai. It should be a source of amazement to modern readers that Nightingale had so little of what we would identify as formal training. What she knew came directly from her brief internship in Germany and from hands-on experience. She arrived in Turkey with a number of unproven theories that have since been proven. And she had only her good intelligence and keen observation to thank.

For instance, she had observed that the practice of "bleeding" patients did more harm than good. Similarly, she disagreed with prescribing opiates, arsenic, and mercury to sick people. All these opinions would be proven correct in laboratory settings over the next decades, but the Barracks Hospital was her chance to put her theories into immediate practice.

She rightly understood that a thorough cleaning was the first priority and quipped that the strongest among her staff would be needed at the wash-tubs. She and her nurses set to work bathing the patients, washing and changing their bed sheets, and, so far as possible, improving the hygiene of the straw beds on which they were destined to languish.

Many of the regimens that Nightingale introduced at Scutari look like mere common sense to modern eyes, so it is important to note that the actions she took in reforming care at the hospital were, at that time, controversial and even revolutionary. A combination of bravery and bravado was required to pull them off.

She developed a triage system that required soldiers to be relieved of all their blood-soaked clothing and bathed immediately upon admittance. She put to a stop the practice of using the same cloth to clean multiple patients. Though it may have bewildered some of her nurses, she insisted that each patient be wiped with a clean cloth, thereby curbing a world of cross-contamination. In the absence of industrial washing machines, she ordered cauldrons of water to be boiled and used to disinfect lice-infested linens and clothes. Prior to

Nightingale's arrival, it had not occurred to the orderlies that full buckets of human waste needed to be removed from the immediate vicinity of the patients and emptied. That changed. The hospital was completely unventilated, so she commanded that windows be installed that allowed the circulation of fresh air. Under her orders, a hired team of local Turks replaced a fire-damaged floor.

Patients were poorly nourished, so Nightingale had a kitchen built, and she once again reached into her own pocket to finance its stores. Soon some hospital staff were diverted to making nourishing and easily digestible food of the classic hospital variety: soup, meat broth, and jellies (the ancestors of gelatin desserts). She also financed several building renovations.

Theft at the Barracks Hospital was rampant prior to Nightingale's arrival. She sent trusted staff members to the Turkish market to buy back goods and supplies that had been siphoned off the hospital and then devised an inventory system to stop further theft.

Within a year, the mortality rate at Barracks Hospital declined dramatically. Nightingale was beloved among the patients and most of the nurses with good reason. She was not only a stellar hospital administrator, but she was also a tireless caregiver. She changed bandages and cleaned wounds right alongside the nurses she supervised. She took a particular interest in hopeless cases that the hospital doctors had declared too far gone to save. Effectively raised in a hothouse, she was amazingly unsqueamish.

The same could not be said of all the hospital doctors. One of them wrote a letter home complaining that Nightingale had dressed the wounds of a soldier in full view of his exposed genitals. Apparently, the doctor cared more about the wounded pride of the soldier than about his actual wounds. Another doctor found it "unladylike" that she observed surgeries with her arms crossed.

She wrote detailed letters to the family members of soldiers who died in her care. These letters show that she understood how important it is for family to know the circumstances of their loved one's death and the events that transpired in the hours before it. She described what the patient ate and his last minute requests. She may have minimized the suffering and exaggerated the heroism of her patients, but it is obvious that her letters were carefully crafted and that she spent considerable time on them.

Nor did Nightingale neglect the basic dignity of her patients. Though it did not prove to save lives, she insisted that surgical procedures be done behind a privacy screen. Previously, they had been conducted in full view of the other patients.

Florence Nightingale cut an impressive figure that appealed to the imaginations of her staff and patients. And soon the British people, waiting at home for the war to end, caught a glimpse of her through word-of-mouth praise that streamed in from returning soldiers. She was slender and graceful, seemingly fragile, but with the stomach of a surgeon and the unflagging energy of an automaton.

It was at the ramshackle Barracks Hospital that the iconic image of the "lady of the lamp" was born. It was Nightingale's practice to patrol the entire hospital by herself at night, checking every single bed and carrying a simple oil lamp to light her way in the dark. She would exchange words with as many as she could and smile at others. The soldiers themselves took such comfort from this simple ritual that it inspired song and rhetoric. One soldier wrote home saying that he and his peers sought to kiss her shadow. A song composed while the war was still waging describes her as "one of heaven's best gifts." A poem by Henry

Wadsworth Longfellow features the line "Lo! in that house of misery/A lady with a lamp I see."

To say that Nightingale's sister, Parthenope, played a part in making Florence famous is not to say that she did not deserve fame. It would have been difficult to find a more effective public relations champion, however. Parthenope published Florence's letters, carefully editing them with the surgical precision of a twenty-first century reputation manager. She cut out graphic details of injury and surgery as well as mundane details that did not make for good narrative. Though Parthenope and her mother had bitterly opposed Florence's ambitions in nursing, things had changed once Florence had taken the plunge and moved out of her parents' house. The Nightingale females were very insistent about the attention that was due them and overly solicitous of Florence's welfare. But they were not a divisive family. They would never denounce her or cut her off. Once her entrance into medicine was an accomplished fact, they really had no choice but to take an active interest and help her in any way they could.

At one point in her Crimea adventure, the commander-in-chief in the Crimea, Lord Raglan, asked Nightingale how her father viewed her pursuit of a career in medicine. In a letter home,

Nightingale largely reinvented her father as a man who, having no sons, was prepared to sacrifice his daughter for the welfare of his country. It is unlikely that William Edward Nightingale, who was quite protective of all his womenfolk, ever told his daughter to come back with her shield or upon it; but in her letter, Nightingale gave him credit for that Spartan sentiment.

Four months into her tenure as superintendent of the Barracks Hospital, Florence Nightingale welcomed a visit and inspection by the Sanitary Commission. At this point in our story, it is worth pausing to consider the part that sanitation played, historically, in medical care. We now take it for granted that hospitals must be scrupulously clean, and if a medical facility fails in its mission to keep the premises sanitary, we assume the health of its patients will suffer.

But in the mid-nineteenth century, the relationship between sanitation and health was not yet a widely accepted notion. The germ theory had not clearly shown how infection and viruses travel from one sick person to another, more rapidly when hands are not washed and shared equipment and possessions are not sterilized.

Current assumptions about sanitation grow out of a "Sanitary Awakening" that began in England in the late eighteenth century. In 1842 the theory of sanitation got a momentous leg up when medical researcher Edwin Chadwick wrote and published a book titled *General Report on the Sanitary Conditions of the Labouring Population of Great Britain.* Chadwick, however, was a controversial figure with a number of powerful naysayers among England's political leadership. Nevertheless, his ideas were so powerful and so well-argued and documented that the theory of sanitation continued its forward momentum.

Nightingale could well have greeted the Sanitation Commission with hostility and resentment. They were, after all, assigned to find and correct sanitation problems and report back on them to the British people. Many hospital administrators would have dodged them so far as possible, attempted to cover up infractions, and made their job as difficult as could be. Nightingale, however, did just the opposite. She recognized that the extensive efforts she had made on behalf of her patients only went so far. She welcomed the infrastructural improvements that the Commission was prepared to make. The gentlemen of the Commission paved the area outside the hospital and introduced a drainage system. They cleaned the aqueduct and implemented a system for flushing the sewers under the hospital with fresh water, thus eliminating the toxic gas that was rising through the hospital's floor. The Commission also disinfected the hospitals walls and improved the air circulation by placing vents in the roof.

The death rate at the Barracks Hospital fell dramatically as a consequence of the combined improvements made by Nightingale herself and the Sanitation Commission. Once the terrible mortality rate had declined, Nightingale found herself free to address the mind and soul of the soldiers under her care, and she set about making many significant improvements to the military.

The men who enlisted in the Victorian Army were a diverse group. Some were from very poor families, and the military was the only real alternative to starvation. Others were the second or third son of wealthy families. Because they would not inherit an estate, these late children were often encouraged to "seek their fortunes" in military service. Other soldiers were simply adventurers with a high excitement threshold and perhaps a dim ability to believe in their own mortality.

No one in Victorian Britain imagined that the military, in a time of war, was anything less than an extremely risky adventure. It was somewhat like playing the lottery. The rewards were potentially very high, but the chances of dying or becoming disabled were much greater. The lot of the common soldier was not improved by his reputation, especially among British politicians. It was not uncommon for British leaders to voice the opinion that soldiers were low-lifes and that the cost of improvements to the military would be wasted.

It is true that alcohol abuse was rampant in the Victorian army. As if their risk of death via injury or infection were not bad enough, some soldiers drank to the point of obliteration. Death by alcohol poisoning was not at all rare. Before Nightingale's advent, even the patients at the Scutari hospital staggered from their sick beds and made their way to the nearest Greek or Turkish saloon.

Nightingale sensibly banned all sale and consumption of alcohol in her hospital, but she did not stop there. She did not buy into the low opinion of the everyday soldier that was common among politicians. She may have made a savvy correlation between drinking and boredom because she started a campaign to improve the education and stimulate the intellect of her patients. Using money provided by her father, Nightingale bought encyclopedias, writing paper, pens, and learning materials related to natural history and geology. Her idea was to replace the need for alcohol with something much, much better: mental stimulation. The higher-ranking army officers were assigned to the study of trigonometry.

Nightingale also believed, correctly as it turned out, that if soldiers could send money home, they would not squander it on drink. The military of the time had in place a system for sending money home through the local paymaster, but it appears that soldiers did not trust that system. They did, however, trust Florence Nightingale. So when she offered to send money home for the soldiers, they took her up on that offer. She asked her uncle Sam Smith to receive these remittances and forward them on to their families. The sharp spike in money sent home inspired the military to set up a more formal system. Acting on Nightingale's example, the war leadership set up post offices in Scutari, Constantinople, and Balaclava by which soldiers could send money home via the postal service. The amount of money sent home was much greater than naysaying politicians predicted. A total of 71,000 pounds in soldier pay found its way to British loved ones using this system. Nightingale quipped that this simple solution "saved money from the canteen."

Her efforts to provide an alternative to getting wasted did not end there. Nightingale set up an alternative entertainment establishment called "Inkerman Cafe." The cafe, situated near a shoreline and benefitting from a sea view, was a sort of coffee shop. Nightingale took a detailed interest in setting up this venue. To make it appealing, she sent provisions of ham, butter, tea urns, and newspapers to be dispersed to soldiers at no cost upon the cafe's opening.

Once she had the Barracks Hospital under control, Nightingale turned her attention to the other military hospitals in the Crimea. When she was sent to redeem the care of wounded soldiers in the Crimean War, Nightingale was vested with considerable authority. She was officially the Superintendent of Nurses. After her success with the Barracks Hospital, she received a further commission as the "Almoner of the free gifts" in British hospitals set up in the Crimea.

This commission came directly from Queen Victoria, who had taken an avid interest in Nightingale's career. Victoria solicited and received information about Nightingale's success, and she took the further step of asking what materials would bring comfort to the wounded who were under Nightingale's care.

Victoria then sent a sort of enormous care packet to Nightingale to be dispersed at her discretion. The packet contained, among other things, warm scarves for nurses. Many civilians followed the example of the queen and sent care packages of clothing, food, and creature comforts to the soldiers overseas. Nightingale was charged with the responsibility for appropriately distributing these gifts where they were needed, and she enlisted the help of military doctors in determining where the gifts should be sent.

Under her two titles, Nightingale toured the other British war hospitals for the last twelve months of the war. Her presence was not always welcomed, nor was her authority to make recommendations universally recognized, despite the enormous responsibility that had been placed on her by both the government and the queen.

Dr. John Hall, a man who believed in performing amputations without the benefit of sedation, was one of the doctors who clashed with Nightingale. Officially, Nightingale was Hall's subordinate, and he resisted her recommendations for improving the hospitals' systems. Hall was at that time the Principal Medical Officer in the Crimea, and his complacency toward appalling hospital conditions was a large factor in the poor perception that the British public back home had formed of the military's care for the wounded. Hall was not an innovator, and he bristled at offers of help, seeing them as insults rather than as sincere attempts at positive change. Nightingale was critical of his policy of promoting nurses that she deemed incompetent. Hall responded by trying to undermine Nightingale's work. In letters home, he labeled her a "petticoat imperieuse."

It appears that he had not taken the measure of Nightingale's enormous popularity back in England or the queen's high regard for her. While her conflict with Hall was raging, Nightingale received a costly brooch as a gift from the queen. This brooch featured the Saint George cross and the words "Crimea" and "Blessed are the merciful." It was designed by none other than Prince Albert, Victoria's husband.

Despite Hall's opposition, Nightingale's recommendations were implemented. Nutrition and sanitation at the hospitals were both improved. She also insisted that soldiers be sent to the hospital immediately upon receiving an injury or demonstrating symptoms of sickness. Previous practice had been to send them to the hospital only when they were so ill that their chances of recovery were marginal.

As far at the folks back home in England were concerned, Nightingale could do no wrong. In the spring of 1856, the War Office issued an official communique that reiterated Nightingale's authority over all the hospitals in the Crimea and on the Bosphorus strait. This action put paid to any insubordination of John Hall and other professionals who had resisted Nightingale's reforms.

Nightingale fever led directly to the launch of the Nightingale Fund, a fund intended to help Nightingale realize her dream of building a permanent nursing school upon her return to England. Campaigners for the Nightingale Fund raised a fortune in donations—equivalent in current currency to several million dollars.

But, in her letters, it is quite clear that the praise that meant the most to her came from Nightingale's immediate family. Her mother, who had fought her tooth and nail to prevent her from becoming a nurse, wrote to say how proud she was of Florence. Parthenope, too, was ecstatic in her praise. Even Florence's father was cautiously admiring of his daughter's wartime effort. In a letter home, Florence said, in effect, that her family's good opinion was worth more than anything. "Life is sweet after all," she noted.

The Crimean War came to an official end on March 30, 1856. The British were nominally the victors when the Treaty of Paris was signed. It was one of the many wars that seem to have made little impression on the whole of history. Perhaps its most important claim to fame was the actualization of Florence Nightingale.

A Call for Reform

Altogether, the British Army lost 20,400 soldiers in the Crimean War. It was a devastating loss, one that decimated Britain's military. This disaster was widely referred to as the "loss of an army." The death of so many men was not mourned only by their families and sweethearts. Mismanagement in Crimea and the consequent death toll also put a serious dent in Britain's economy just at the moment when the industrial revolution needed able-bodied manufacturing employees.

But the real scandal was that sixteen thousand of those deaths were due to illness and neglect. Only 2,600 soldiers died in actual battle, and another 1,800 died of injuries sustained in combat with the enemy.

Such a loss was impossible for the British government to gloss over, no matter how lowly the status of the everyday foot soldier. A carefully compiled report—written by Colonel Alexander Tulloch and Scottish surgeon John McNeill—implicated military management for the death of so many men. The McNeill–Tulloch report showed how food shortages occurred when food could have been purchased within a few miles of most military encampments. It castigated the condition of hospitals to which sick men were sent and the treatment they received.

However, Britain's political leaders did, effectively, conspire in a cover-up. The report was repudiated by the country's war secretary, Lord Panmure, and documentation exists to suggest that even Queen Victoria conspired to suppress the report as well as any inquiry into the wrongdoings of military leadership. The British Army was, at that point in time, at least partly under the authority of the Queen, who feared both for her popularity and for the reputation of the army. Meanwhile, four military leaders who were perhaps most at fault for the worst disasters in the Crimea were feted, decorated, and congratulated for their success.

Nightingale was one of the last people to return home from the war, and she made her way home covertly, first stopping over at a London convent where she spent some time reconciling the account of her expenditures in the east.

The Nightingale Fund stood ready for Nightingale to implement her dream of starting up a truly first-class training institute for nurses. It was a dream that had been dear to Nightingale prior to her war service. But the war had changed that dream: Nightingale now had a taste for hospital management. Teaching held less charm than before.

As soon as she arrived back in England, she received considerable pressure to report on conditions in the military and make recommendations for improvement. For several months, she held back from doing so. Nightingale had succeeded almost single-handedly in rescuing the profession of nursing from its terrible reputation. When she returned to England, nursing had become respectable, largely due to the great publicity her efforts in the Crimea had received. She was, understandably, concerned that a strident renunciation of war leadership and management would draw undesirable attention to the nursing field. In a letter, she wrote that nursing would need to remain a profession of quiet and unthanked service, not an endeavor where employees would expect accolades or public recognition.

But several circumstances came together to change her mind. One was a private meeting with Queen Victoria. Nightingale and the queen had enjoyed a relationship of mutual admiration while Nightingale was serving the crown in Turkey. So Nightingale formed the idea that she should make a private report to the queen about what she had seen in the Crimea. During their meeting, however, it became obvious to Nightingale that the queen had no honest intention to correct abuses within the military. That meeting and the suppression of the McNeill–Tulloch report finally drove Nightingale to demand an inquiry. War Secretary Lord Panmure agreed to Nightingale's demand for a royal commission to investigate the management of the war.

Nightingale set about in earnest to write an honest report on what she had observed in Crimea. She did not attempt to write the report using only her own knowledge. She assembled a team that included Alexander Tulloch and John McNeill, the authors of the discredited earlier report. She also sought and received the assistance of William Farr. Farr was a brilliant statistician at a point in history when statistics was a relatively new discipline. Under Farr's tutelage, Nightingale found that she, too, had a flair for numbers. Nightingale made use of Farr's handy "deaths per one thousand people" percentage to make some of her points. In writing her report on the war, Nightingale also invented what is today known as the pie chart, which she referred to as a "coxcomb." Nightingale used graphics and charts successfully because she understood how they could be used to make information accessible to a wide range of people, including those who did not know how to read.

Farr's influence on Nightingale should not be underestimated. Not only did he persuade her of the value of statistics, but he also helped convince her that poor hygiene, more than poor nutrition and exhaustion, accounted for much of the high death toll in the Crimea.

We must remember how very little scientific training Nightingale had before undertaking the supervision of wartime hospitals. Most of what she learned of science was absorbed after her adventure in the Crimea, during the months that she had available to study and learn and make conclusions about what had happened during the war. Nightingale had always been far ahead of her time in observing the importance of hygiene, but she had very little scientific foundation for her belief in cleanliness. Farr helped her with the science.

Nightingale was haunted by the number of soldiers who died under her watch in the first three months of her tenure in Scutari. When she applied Farr's statistics to her time at the Barracks Hospital, she found that she could attribute much of the decline in soldier mortality to the improvements made by the Sanitation Commission. She also came to believe in Farr's theory of "zymotics." Though the transmission of germs was not yet understood, Farr developed the theory of zymotics to explain why patients who were crowded together were more likely to die or worsen than patients who were kept at a distance from one another.

While Florence was occupied with her post-mortem of wartime hospitals, her father, William Edward Nightingale, made an unsuccessful run for Parliament. His principal claim to fame was as the father of the now-famous Florence Nightingale. That tenuous platform was not enough to win the voters, however, and he lost the election. In a letter to his daughter, he acknowledged that his student had far exceeded her teacher. He notes, with some self-pity, that he had failed to make a name for himself and that she was his "only genius."

Nightingale had become a celebrated heroine during her time in the Crimea, so it is important to understand how brave she had to be to use her own hospital, the Barracks Hospital in Scutari, as an object lesson in failed hygiene. In her report, she noted the high death rate in the Scutari hospital during her first winter as the Superintendent of Nursing in the Crimea, and she did not flinch from reporting that injured soldiers who stayed shivering in the field had stood a better chance of survival. She gave no credit to herself for the improvements in hygiene that she had made; instead, her report directed all credit to the Sanitation Commission.

Nightingale became justifiably convinced that good hospital design was an essential ingredient in patient recovery. The design of the Barracks Hospital made it more or less a death trap, she concluded. She decided that it was important to identify who was responsible for authorizing the former Turkish barracks as a hospital, and her research led at first to her old nemesis, John Hall. Hall had signed off on the use of the barracks, but Nightingale became convinced that neither he nor his fellow doctors had sufficient knowledge or training to judge the efficacy of a hospital building. When she followed the paper trail further up, she found that it led to her old friend Sir Sidney Herbert, the very man who had appointed her to leadership in Crimea. Regretfully, Nightingale identified Herbert as the man most responsible for the horrific British death toll in the Crimea.

Despite a debilitating illness, in 1857 Nightingale completed her report on the state of war-time medical care, and she hoped that it would be published in its entirety by the Royal Commission that had been formed, at her request, to conduct an investigation. That was not to be, however. Instead, her report was suppressed. Only fragments of Nightingale's findings found their way into the commission's final published report. Nightingale's report had originally been solicited as a "confidential report" to the Prime Minister, Lord Palmerston. As such, she was not at liberty to publish it without the government's consent, but it is clear she regretted that her report did not find its way to the general public. She printed several copies and sent them to friends with instructions not to pass them along. Eventually, after her death, some of those copies found their way into libraries. The failure of the British government to publish Nightingale's report may have cost incalculable lives. One historian has theorized that, if Nightingale's findings on sanitation and care for the sick had been more widely known, hundreds of thousands of lives could have been saved during America's Civil War.

Beginning in 1857, Nightingale was very sick and often bedridden. There's a certain irony to the fact that her illness was never properly diagnosed, and she remained in poor health to the end of her life. Some biographers have speculated that she was a hypochondriac, though she hardly fits the profile. Other, more recent books on Nightingale have proposed that she suffered from brucellosis, a disease discovered in the twentieth century. It can be successfully treated with antibiotics that were, of course, unavailable in Nightingale's time. If Nightingale had brucellosis, it is likely that she contracted it by consuming contaminated milk or meat while serving in the Crimea. Interestingly, no biographer has suggested that Nightingale might have suffered from post-traumatic stress disorder.

Nightingale did not move back in with her family during her illness but, rather, maintained an independent residence in Mayfair's Burlington Hotel. She did, however, benefit from her family's resources. Harley Street specialists were located and dispatched to her side. Family funds paid for trips to the Malvern Spa.

Individualism

From 1856 on, Nightingale became increasingly committed to the ideal of individualism, a principle that was taught both in the Unitarian Church in which she grew up and by Harriet Martineau, the legendary journalist whom Nightingale had befriended in her hour of need.

Nightingale's letters from this period betray an increasing alienation from her family. She felt that their newfound admiration for her was prompted by her popularity and not because they truly supported her ideas or the cause of reform. Where she had been transformed by life experiences, they had stayed the same. The exception to her mistrust was her Aunt Mai. Mai had accompanied her to the Crimea and proved of real service. It was to her that Nightingale turned for help with her correspondence. Mai would take an increasingly larger role in Nightingale's life as the heroine of the Crimea aged, and she often acted as a buffer between Florence and the rest of her family.

In 1857 Nightingale's health took a nose-dive. She couldn't sleep, couldn't eat, and was frequently nauseated. Her doctor's prescription was a water cure, much like the one her father had undertaken. She made her way to Malvern spa, where a medical team deduced that her main health issue was exhaustion. Mai colluded with Florence in keeping her illness a secret from her family. Nightingale's letters from this period show that she feared she would die without having accomplished what she set out to do. She was the famous "lady with a lamp" to everyone but herself. She saw herself not as the British public did, but as someone thwarted in her goals.

In the midst of her illness, life threw Nightingale a curve ball in the form of a fifty-seven-year-old suitor. Florence herself was thirty-seven, well past the age when well-bred Victorian ladies were supposed to dream of love and marriage. She had already dismissed a would-be husband who seemed perfect for her; now she was mostly bedridden and increasingly eccentric.

Despite all of that, she was intensely interesting to Sir Harry Verney, a wealthy, widowed philanthropist and Member of Parliament. Verney had learned of Nightingale, as the rest of Britain had, from newspaper reports of her work in the Crimea. No doubt, he saw in her a kindred spirit—someone who, like himself, yearned to design a better world. Like her, he was interested in education and rural health.

It must be acknowledged that, in approaching Nightingale, Verney was a perfect gentleman. He wrote first, asking if he could introduce her to his daughters. An invitation was extended, and he met her, daughters in tow, at the Burlington. Nightingale was, indeed, interested in Verney's ideas, but she had by now unapologetically committed herself to a single life. In Verney she saw an opportunity not for herself, but for her unaccountably still-single sister Parthenope. The introduction was made, and Verney was successfully redirected. The two were married less than a year later, with the joyful blessing of parents and sister. Verney remained useful to Nightingale as a political consultant and ally.

By the end of the year, she rallied. She had eluded death, but not the weakness and tendency to fatigue that plagued her to varying degrees for the rest of her life. She refused to give up her efforts at reform, so she engineered her life and household so that she could continue her work as a reformer and activist despite her ongoing weakness. Nightingale had been living in the Burlington Hotel, but now she moved into the hotel's annex, a change that allowed her the use of a relatively spacious apartment with a large upstairs bedroom, a maid's room, a dressing room, a guest bedroom, and a living room, which she adamantly refused to call a "drawing room." Drawing rooms were the sphere of wealthy and well-connected women. As Nightingale saw it, they represented everything that was wrong with Victorian life and a thinking woman's place in it. When her well-intentioned father tried to send her some drawing-room furnishings, she replied that she did not have one and that drawing rooms had already been the ruin of far too many women.

Though she remained unmarried for the rest of her life and never permanently shared her apartment with another human, she found companionship in a family of Persian cats. They were the gift of her old friend and mentor Mary Clarke and her husband Julius von Mohl. Clarke, the ardent feminist, had become a bride in her fifties. The cats provided exactly the right amount of distraction from Nightingale's crusades. They provided an excuse to be whimsical. In her letters, Nightingale wrote, tongue in cheek, that she had tried to provide respectable "husbands" for her cats, but they preferred the low company of alley cats. These beloved pets marched across her work station, dipping their paws in ink that was still wet on the page and leaving paw prints on important papers. They reminded Nightingale that life is not always deadly serious.

Illness never stopped Nightingale. She was famous, and she was influential; so if she required that meetings take place in her apartment, that's where they took place. She summoned activists and parliamentary members, and they heeded the call. While scarcely leaving her quarters, she continued to shape history for the next several decades.

We know that Nightingale was tremendously influential because historians can draw clear connections between her writings and certain reforms that were made in her lifetime. We may never be able to measure the exact degree of her influence, however, because she did so much work behind the scenes. Though she did write and publish prolifically under her own name, she often preferred to make a quiet remark in the ear of the right person. She was, among other things, a ghostwriter. She wrote countless articles about the state of the medical field and army medicine and then gave them freely away to other writers and journalists. If they put their own names on them and took the credit, so much the better, so long as her ideas made their flight.

For several hours a day, she met with Sir Sidney Herbert, who had retained his seat in Parliament despite a regime change that had toppled several other leaders. As needed, she reclined on a couch to preserve her energy during these conversations. She also conferred extensively with a new ally, Dr. John Sutherland. Like Nightingale, Sutherland was a reformer and a believer in sanitation. Sutherland served a dual role in Nightingale's life. He helped her with her writing, often providing marginal notes on drafted work, which was enormously useful when she was writing *Notes on Nursing*. He also acted as her doctor. Like the doctors at Malvern, he diagnosed her with overwork and recommended rest, but he wasn't very successful at getting her to comply. When she overdid it to the point that she was shaking, he would intervene and administer what care he could.

Nightingale was frustrated with the government's reluctance to implement the military reforms that she and other specialists had advocated. In her impatience, she turned to her old friend Harriet Martineau. Like Nightingale, Martineau was a household name. She was most famous for writing and publishing a book titled *Illustrations of Political Economy*. Nightingale rightly believed that she could leverage Martineau's power as a journalist to make the public aware of the need for army reform.

Nightingale therefore sent Martineau a copy of her latest book on army hospital administration. Martineau agreed that the subject was newsworthy, so she set to work on a series of articles that appeared in the *Daily News*. Nightingale agreed to review them for accuracy. Nightingale gave Martineau a plethora of notes and papers, which became the backbone of Martineau's book *England and Her Soldiers*. It told the story of Nightingale's experience in Scutari, not holding back the grim details of high mortality and poor hospital design. *England and Her Soldiers* argued for the preventative health measures that Nightingale so fiercely advocated, especially nutrition and hygiene. The book featured graphs that Nightingale had created, and Nightingale functioned as an unnamed collaborator and bottom line editor.

When Martineau's publishers offered her a pittance for her hard work, Nightingale stepped in and granted the author a private stipend to supplement her income. The high cost of printing threatened the book's distribution, so Nightingale gifted Martineau with printing blocks that facilitated mass production. She also encouraged Martineau to lower the price of the book so as to increase sales. Nightingale felt that *England and Her Soldiers* told a story that needed to be told, but the British Army did not like to hear or read criticism of itself and attempted to suppress the book. When army officials refused to accept books that Nightingale sent at her own expense, she paid a book distributor to get them into the reading rooms of the common soldier.

By 1861 it was clear that Nightingale's multi-level activism had paid off. Though it would be untenable to suggest that she alone was responsible for the tremendous reforms that took place in medicine and in the military, she was the clear leader of the reforming vanguard. By 1861 sanitation in military barracks and hospitals was greatly improved. Military facilities were better lighted and better ventilated. Drinking water was safe, and attention was paid to how water and other waste was removed from the premises. An Army Statistics Department, charged with providing data on soldier welfare, was established, and it was soon destined to become the best of its kind in Europe.

Nightingale's dream of an Army Medical School was also realized, and she had a guiding hand in its development. Nightingale hand-picked several of the faculty from amongst her fellow Crimean War veterans. Nightingale also wrote the school's bylaws as well as a number of syllabi and lessons. These innovations bore solid fruit. The mortality rate of soldiers stationed in England fell more than fifty percent. Britain's soldiers started surviving, rather than succumbing to, the perils of dysentery, typhus, cholera, and tuberculosis. Nightingale and her team of moral soldiers had prevailed.

New Hospitals, New Nurses

One lesson Nightingale had learned in Scutari was that a poorly designed hospital was a death trap. The very design of the Barracks Hospital, with its overcrowded corridors, inadequate ventilation, and non-existent drainage, was guilty of thousands of soldiers' deaths. Unfortunately, the average civilian hospital back home in Britain was not much better. "Modern" hospitals were designed and built on the model of a big house. No thought went into air circulation or containing infections. As in Scutari, patients were lined up in corridors, toilets and sinks were substandard even for the time, and lighting was poor.

In 1859 Nightingale wrote and published a book titled *Notes on Hospitals*, which called for radical innovations in hospital design. Much of this book is devoted to inculcating better ventilation. The hospitals of the future, Nightingale insisted, should not have windows on only one side. Instead, windows should be placed on all sides to enable cross-ventilation. She called for high ceilings and for windows to extend in height to within a foot of the ceiling. She condemned the practice of coming into a patient's room and closing the shutters and drawing the drapes—a mistake she had seen both doctors and nurses commit. While many doctors seemed to believe that patients should be spared the cruelty of natural light,

Nightingale insisted that each patient had the right to it and that no beds should be stationed in a room without windows.

Notes on Hospitals also demands that toilets and sinks be in good working order, along with drainage systems. Waste water should not be allowed to linger on the premises. Nightingale went on to demand that floors, ceilings, and walls should be constructed of cement rather than absorbent materials that suck up and retain dirt and infectious matter. Furthermore, these surfaces should all be white so that anyone could quickly judge whether they were clean or not. Laundry rooms needed more space and enough water to allow the washer women to do their work properly without themselves becoming sick. Perhaps most importantly, patients should not be crowded together so that sickness spreads from one patient to another. Nightingale advocated a "pavilion" style of hospital construction, with wings that allowed patients to be segregated according to their illness.

Nightingale acknowledged that the cost of land and new construction would be high. Therefore, because land in the city was so costly, she recommended that new hospitals be built in the suburbs, where land was more affordable.

Nightingale's ideas about hospital design were enormously influential. Victorian biographer Lytton Strachey went so far as to say that, after Nightingale published *Notes on Hospitals*, every newly built hospital reflected her influence. The first hospital to be built on Nightingale's plan was the general hospital in Woolwich, England, which was opened in 1865, only six short years after the publication of Nightingale's book. The hospital at Woolwich quickly became the standard for new hospitals throughout Britain and other parts of the world.

A few short years later, Prince Albert contacted Nightingale on behalf of Dom Pedro V, the king of Portugal, who wished to model a new hospital on Nightingale's principles. With her usual sense of mission, Nightingale dove into the work of advising on this project. She scoured the plans and corresponded at length with the king's architect. Well into the project, she learned to her chagrin that the king had intended this to be a children's hospital. Much of the design needed to be altered, but Nightingale went back to the drawing board and designed a hospital that was suitable for children.

Nightingale's book on hospitals may ultimately have been her most important contribution to letters, but her next book, *Notes on Nursing: What It Is, and What It Is Not*, became her most popular. It was published in 1859 in England, and an American edition came out the next year. In *Notes on Nursing,* Nightingale introduced many of the ideas from her suppressed report. She managed to take the list of egregious mistakes made in the war and turn them into a helpful set of proactive recommendations for care of the sick. *Notes on Nursing* remained so relevant through the ensuing decades that it was reissued in 1974.

Nightingale's book starts right out with stressing the importance of ventilation and then moves on to outline what a "health house" should look like. By "health house," Nightingale basically meant any medical treatment facility. Nightingale's well-constructed health house featured clean air, clean water, clean facilities, good drainage, and good lighting. In her chapters on feeding the sick, she noted the need to make sure that patients get enough to eat. If a patient is too weak to eat solid food, soft food or broth must be available. She also observed that some patients cannot tolerate eggs or anything made with eggs. She cautioned nurses that patients need a balance of meat and vegetables. Though this seems a self-evident point today, at the time, patients were often fed meat to the exclusion of all else.

In *Notes on Nursing*, Nightingale stressed that medicine and medical professionals should first do no harm—a principle that still very much guides the health industry.

Notes on Nursing not only addressed the essential physical requirements that all patients have in common, but it also offered suggestions for their psychological welfare. Patients should, so far as possible, be comforted with sunlight, colors, books, and even pets. It may be worth noting that, in recent times, nursing homes are discovering the value of therapy cats and dogs—which shows how on-target Nightingale was about the psychological aspects of recovery.

After writing *Notes on Hospitals* and *Notes on Nursing*, it was time for Nightingale to do something about the Nightingale Fund, a considerable sum of money that had been set aside for a nursing school. The nursing school had been a long-time dream of Nightingale, but dreams change, and she now wished to beg off. To that end, she pleaded ill health and asked Sidney Herbert to release her from any obligation to start up this new school. Herbert demurred, however. After all, Nightingale was the face of nursing, and without her involvement, he did not think the project would succeed. A compromise was forged. Nightingale would remain invested, but a subcommittee was formed to steer the project, and a secretary was hired to manage day-to-day details and paperwork.

Nightingale did not want to manage the new school, so she cast about for someone to whom she could delegate responsibility. She believed that Sarah Elizabeth Wardroper, the nursing superintendent of London's St. Thomas's Hospital, was the perfect candidate. Like Nightingale, she had little actual nurse training; her genius was for hospital administration. Before departing for the Crimea, Nightingale had recruited several nurses from Wardroper's stable.

There was also the question of where the nursing school should be located. Nightingale believed that it needed to be embedded within a hospital, but a new training program had the potential to disrupt a hospital that was already well run. Nightingale's goal was to introduce a nurse training program that would make its host hospital better, not worse. St. Thomas's Hospital offered the perfect opportunity.

St. Thomas's was already in trouble. It was dilapidated, and it also lay directly in the path of a railway line that had yet to be built. Officials were debating whether to bulldoze the entire facility or just the buildings that were directly in the way of future trains. Through the interventions of Nightingale, it was decided that the hospital would be moved, in its entirety to a new location. Meanwhile, the nurse training program would be started up in the old facility.

The Nightingale School of Nursing, which was launched in 1860, was set up as a four-year program in which the trainees would mostly learn by doing. During their first year, "probationers" would receive training, and in the next three years, they went to work in a hospital or medical facility that served the poor. Students signed four-year contracts.

Not everyone was a fan. One surgeon in particular was critical of the new training program. He published a contemptuous rant in which he averred that nurses did no more than administering poultices (hot or cold cloth compresses). They were basically housemaids, he went on, and they rarely committed themselves to any institution for long. As such, they needed little to no real training.

He could not have been more wrong. The nurses in the Nightingale program learned a wide array of skills, most of which fill the skill set of today's nurses: bandaging wounds, giving enemas, turning patients over to help them avoid bed sores, helping patients relearn the skill of walking and using their other limbs, monitoring ventilation in patient rooms, and making close observation of patients' breathing, eating, elimination, and reactions to medication. The trainees attended lectures where they were expected to take notes and, to ensure accountability, their notes were reviewed. They took regular examinations. They wore tidy brown dresses with contrastive white caps and aprons. They were required to keep their hairstyles simple.

The Nightingale School of Nursing was not the very first nurse training program, but it was the first secular program. Nightingale continued to feel that, to become a respectable profession, nursing must be divorced from religion. That does not mean, however, that the nurses in training in her school were allowed any moral laxity. Quite the contrary— Nightingale's trainees were held to the highest standards of propriety. They were expected to be punctual, quiet, sober, clean, trustworthy, and respectful to doctors. Students were graded not just on their mastery of their subject, but also on their character.

Though her precarious health did not allow Nightingale to supervise the workings of the school in person, she found a way to supervise from her rooms at the Burlington: Every month, each trainee was assigned to write a detailed report of one day's study and work. These reports were assigned on a surprise basis to prevent students from presenting a skewed view of their work. Nightingale read these reports carefully and made notes on them in her own writings. Using these documents as well as reports submitted by Wardrop, Nightingale graded each student and submitted a monthly report on her progress.

To fill the seats in her school, Nightingale recruited the daughters of farmers and tradesmen—young women who would otherwise have become shopkeepers, farm wives, or servants. She preferred women who were twenty-five or older, and some of the students were in their thirties. By today's standards, the terms of their nursing education were highly favorable. They paid no tuition, received free room and board (including the requisite English tea), and when they had completed their first year of training, they received a small salary for the remaining three years.

Their accommodations were more than decent. The trainees lived communally on the top floor of St. Thomas's, but each woman had her own bedroom. This nurse hostel was furnished with comfortable chairs, books, wall art, and flowers. The flowers were a gift from Nightingale from her family estate in Embley where they were picked every week and delivered to the nurse hostel.

Despite these excellent terms, however, the program struggled in its first years. Quite a few trainees failed to live up to Nightingale's high moral standards and were dismissed for insubordination or drinking. It was not Nightingale's intention to perpetuate negative stereotypes of nursing. Only a handful of trainees successfully completed the program in its infancy.

The Nightingale School of Nursing was not immediately successful in sending trained professionals into hospitals and group homes where expert medical care was desperately needed. It was, however, enormously successful in providing a model of secular training for nurses. In the years immediately following the launch of the Nightingale school, other such schools were opened, leading to professionalization of the nursing field.

India

The rebellion against British rule in India provided a nearly perfect canvas for Florence Nightingale's reforming instincts. British soldiers were in peril; dead bodies were lying in the streets and spreading contagion; and two million indigenous Indian civilians were living in primitive conditions with little to no education about the importance of sanitation, clean water, and good drainage.

When Nightingale learned in 1857 about the Indian uprising against British dominion, her first instinct was to rise from her bed, killing brucellosis notwithstanding, and go back into the field. Sidney Herbert talked her out of it and persuaded her to do what she did best: stay at home, study the facts, and make world-changing recommendations.

In 1861, while she was writing her recommendations for better sanitation in India, Nightingale lost a great ally. Sidney Herbert, the man who had entrusted her with the entire nursing operation in the Crimea, died of kidney failure. Nightingale's grief was genuine. He had been both a friend and probably her most important collaborator in bringing about the reform of military medicine.

Nightingale herself continued to suffer from a myriad of health issues, which included depression. Beginning in 1861, she also experienced excruciating spinal pain. Nightingale's father may have believed that a nicer residence would improve Florence's health. Whether or not that was his motivation, he rented a house for her on London's South Street. It had great views of Hyde Park on one side and Dorchester House Hotel gardens on the other. The house was lit by ample natural light, and Nightingale was comforted by the sound of birdsong. Within this comfortable setting, she could be found reclined on a chaise lounge, reading a government blue book. She mostly wore black dresses and white lace head-scarves.

Perhaps the best thing about Nightingale's new residence, however, was the proximity of her sister Parthenope and brother-in-law Harry Verney, who lived just a few doors down. Age and illness had softened Nightingale's attitude toward Parthenope. The two entered a new phase of their relationship that was characterized by friendship and kindness. Parthe and Harry also picked up the social slack for Nightingale. When Florence had guests, entertaining them beyond the confines of her own walls was difficult to impossible because of her ongoing illness. Fortunately, Parthe and Harry stepped in and escorted these guests to the opera, the park, the theater, and the

Houses of Parliament. They hosted Nightingale's guests in their home for dinners and teas.

For two years, Nightingale worked diligently on the India Sanitary Commission report. She amassed two vanloads of information and statistics on the state of the British military encampments by sending carefully constructed questionnaires to British military leaders stationed all over India. It is a testament to her influence that two-thirds of the commanders she petitioned sent back their questionnaires, fully completed. The resulting paperwork took up an entire room in Nightingale's house.

The 2,028-page report was issued in 1863 and contained some shocking information. The death rate of British soldiers stationed in India was almost seven percent per year, significantly higher than the death rate of soldiers stationed in Britain in the years prior to reform. The loss of British soldiers in India was almost entirely attributable to poor sanitation. Very few soldiers were actually dying of natural causes.

The high rate of soldier mortality stemmed from causes that were entirely familiar to Nightingale from her sojourn in the Crimea. No thought was given to where camps should be set up.

Soldiers were quartered on sites that featured cholera-infested water and no drainage. Tests of water purity had become available, and Nightingale noted that the average soldier's drinking water contained a hefty quantum of chloride, nitrates, silica, as well as animal products and vegetable matter. Furthermore, soldiers were stuffed into lodgings at the rate of three hundred men per room. The lodgings themselves made the Scutari Barracks look like a palace. A typical military camp would be constructed on a bare earth floor, which was then shellacked with cow manure.

Nightingale had finished her report, and it was scheduled for presentation to Parliament when George Lewis, the Secretary of State for War, died suddenly. Nightingale had maintained a close relationship with the war office; her South Street residence was even chosen for its proximity to the office. She was understandably concerned that Lewis' replacement should be someone friendly to the ideas of sanitation and reform.

Nightingale thought highly of Lord de Grey since they had worked together on several projects, including the launch of the Army Medical School. Nightingale engineered a multi-level campaign to have de Grey appointed to War Secretary. She enlisted Harriet Martineau, as she had done before. Martineau obliged by endorsing de Grey's appointment in her *Daily News* column. Nightingale penned and sent a private letter to the Prime Minister recommending de Grey as Lewis' replacement. She prevailed, and de Grey became the new Secretary of State for War.

The exhaustive report on health concerns in India nearly suffered a death blow when a minor official charged with printing it took it upon himself to abridge the document severely. Vital information was hatcheted out of the report, and the result was a confusing mess of rhetoric that made frequent references to information that had been deleted. Nightingale and her colleagues were outraged. Fortunately, a limited edition of the original 2,000-plus-page report had been printed. However, these precious definitive versions had been sent to the Burial Office, where they were in imminent danger of being burned by the same clerk who had abridged the report.

In a Hail Mary effort to save all her hard work from the fire, Nightingale wrote to every Member of Parliament with whom she was acquainted, advising them to request a copy of the original report from the Burial Office. Many of them complied and thereby rescued the book from destruction.

Nightingale was justifiably concerned that her report would do little good if it found its way only into the hands of Parliament. People living and working in India needed this information more desperately than did the leaders of Britain who were living safely in the home country. To make sure that her report was distributed in India, she offered to underwrite the printing costs, as she had done for Harriet Martineau's book. This offer was gratefully accepted; but before the book could be printed, Nightingale spent a solid three months rewriting the abridged version to correct its mistakes and omissions. This was the version that was distributed in India.

Angered by the hatchet job that was done on Nightingale's original report, two of her long-time friends and colleagues privately printed one section of the India report, which had been titled "Observations." This book, too, found its way to India, where it may ultimately have been more influential that the fuller report. "Observations" became extremely popular, possibly because its short length and numerous illustrations made it readily accessible. Readers referred to it by the nickname "The Little Red Book" because of its red cloth cover.

The two reports circulating through India found critics in high places. Some military and medical leaders were predictably insulted that these reports gave them no credit for improvements they believed they had already made. One Colonel Baker, stationed at the India Office, accused Nightingale of exaggeration. The Chairman of the Bombay Sanitary Commission questioned the accuracy of the reports' statistics. Nightingale made a point of responding to all such reactions. As always, she argued her case with facts heavily infused with salt and irony.

Because Nightingale's health did not permit her to go to India, she needed somebody she could count on to implement her recommendations there. To that end, she approached Sir John Lawrence, who had been recently appointed as the new viceroy in India. Ten days before he was schedule to sail for India, the two of them met at Nightingale's house for several hours. She plied him with ideas and arguments about needed improvements in India. Luckily, Lawrence was unmoved by criticisms of Nightingale's India report. If anything, he felt she had understated the problems. He kept up a correspondence with Nightingale. When he arrived in India, he immediately implemented some of Nightingale's recommendations: sanitary commissions were established in Calcutta, Madras, and Bombay.

Prompted by the viceroy's need and a direct request from Lord de Grey, Nightingale wrote a report titled *Suggestions in Regard to Sanitary Works Required for the Improvement of Indian Stations*. In this pamphlet, Nightingale directed the leaders of the newly formed sanitary commissions to implement better health and hygiene gradually in military encampments and hospitals and in the towns nearby. It is clear that she meant for good hygiene to filter down to the villages of India, where it was also needed.

Where military leaders heeded Nightingale's advice, the results were nearly miraculous. Hugh Rose, the commander-in-chief of the Indian army, implemented Nightingale's advice to grow small-scale gardens in military bases. The soldiers worked these gardens themselves and grew their own food. At one station, an entire battalion of soldiers saved themselves from a cholera epidemic by growing their own food as Nightingale had recommended. Cholera had hit that station so hard that the outgoing soldiers told those incoming that they should not expect to make it out alive. The soldiers who grew and ate their own uncontaminated produce did not contract cholera, however—they did make it out alive.

Nightingale's recommendations to soldiers living in India went beyond basic health and hygiene issues. In the Crimea, she had seen how lifestyle choices could be just as damaging as infection. She believed that soldiers stationed in India would make better choices regarding their money and their free time if they had more opportunities. She recommended the implementation of banks where soldiers could put money into savings, libraries, and recreation areas. Meanwhile, she strongly discouraged drinking. Many military leaders took these recommendations to heart and created a better infrastructure for saving and for wholesome recreation. A new law was passed that imposed a steep fine for selling alcohol near military encampments.

Nightingale did not at first oppose British rule in India, but in 1863 she wrote a paper arguing that the British had a duty to India—one that was not, so far, being honored. This paper, directly enough titled "How People May Live and Not Die In India," argued that the British should not consider India a mere tool for commerce. The British must sow the seeds of civilization, and by 'civilization' she meant "better hygiene." To think otherwise was to abandon morality, she concluded. Her paper was read at the National Social Science Association meeting in Edinburgh by her colleague Dr. Scoresby Jackson.

Nightingale's vigilant campaigns for better health and hygiene in India paid off over time. By 1873 British soldier mortality in India had declined to 1.8 percent from 6.9 percent as a direct result of improved sanitation. Sir Bartle Frere, who became the Governor of Bombay years after the India reports were published, admitted that the little red book had provoked a savage reaction at first, but that it did India a world of good.

Over the years, Nightingale's stance on British involvement in India shifted. She rightly perceived that Britain's dominion became increasingly brutal and exploitative in the face of Indian fervor for independence. By 1878 Nightingale was effectively mobilized in favor of Indian independence. Like Gandhi, she deplored the British tax on salt in India, the abusive conduct of absentee English landlords who forced their Indian tenants into penury, and the British indifference to famine and drought that wiped out masses of rural Indians.

Her article "The People of India," published in the start-up magazine *Nineteenth Century*, stirred up a great deal of sympathy in England for the plight of the exploited Indian national. She followed up the success of "The People of India" with three articles that ran in *Good Words* magazine. In these articles, she not only reiterated her concerns about hygiene and famine, but she also condemned the practice of predatory lending that was rampant in India and the practice of deforestation, which led to flooding.

However, Nightingale was never so immersed in the welfare of India that she became blind to domestic problems a few streets away from her comfortable London home. One of the worst problems plaguing British health care during Nightingale's time was the institution of workhouses. Originally developed to provide shelter to the homeless, workhouses in Nightingale's time had effectively become hospitals. The Poor Law Amendment Act of 1834 stated in so many words that workhouses should be inhospitable places so as to discourage able-bodied people from applying for aid via the workhouse system. The Poor Law was successful insofar as no one who had any other option would go there. But seriously ill people are unable to work, so the workhouses filled up with sick people who could not support themselves.

Workhouses were not quality medical care facilities. People were piled into them without any attempt to segregate the insane or senile from the rest of the population. Similarly, the infectious were allowed to mingle with the uninfected, and standards of hygiene were virtually non-existent. In Nightingale's opinion, workhouses provided no credible medical care for poor people. She was particularly incensed by the failure of workhouses to care for sick children. The workhouse system was just as indifferent to a sick child as it was to a middle-aged slacker, and no attempt was made to separate or protect children from the workhouse population at large.

In collaboration with two colleagues, Nightingale drafted a letter outlining several reforms that needed to be made to the workhouse program. She called for a centralized administration, better funding through tax levy, and separation of children, elderly, sick people, and those with mental illness from the general population. These proposals became the backbone of the Metropolitan Poor Act of 1867. Under this act, children were removed from workhouses and placed in more appropriate institutions.

Nurse Training Stumbles, but Indian Nationalism Gains Allies

Through the 1870s, Nightingale's health continued to be poor. She limited the number of visitors that she would receive. Among those who received a polite decline was the Queen of Holland. She excused herself from many social obligations but found it virtually impossible to excuse herself from any important work. It is difficult to imagine somebody who got more done from a chaise lounge than Florence Nightingale. When her expertise was needed, she always gave the project her full attention—against the advice of Dr. Sutherland, who continued to care for her and collaborate with her simultaneously.

Nightingale believed that her parents would outlive her, so it was a terrible shock to learn that her father, who was in good health at the age of eighty, had died from a fall on the staircase in 1874. Though she had, in the past, criticized her father's lack of greater purpose, she was genuinely grieved to lose him. In her letters, she praised his treatment of his tenants. Where other estate owners allowed their tenants to live in abject poverty, that was never the case on the Nightingale estates, where cottagers lived in clean and well-maintained properties.

The death of William Edward Nightingale somewhat derailed his daughter, who now found herself responsible for a mother who had become blind and senile. The Nightingale estate was entailed away from the female line, which meant that Frances, Florence, and Parthenope Nightingale were disinherited. Frances, Florence's mother, could no longer count on living at Embley, and the income that Florence had received from her father was no longer guaranteed. The heir to the Nightingale estate was William Shore Smith, the son of Aunt Mai, Florence's beloved aunt and WEN's sister. Florence had watched William Shore grow up. She was eleven years his senior, and she had, as was her wont, nursed him through a bout of illness.

To everyone's great relief, Smith turned out to be a generous man. Frances was allowed to live on at the Nightingale's estates, and Smith not only continued Florence's support but also raised her income to two thousand pounds a year, a lavish sum in those times. During the transition, however, Nightingale was called upon to relocate servants and inventory family possessions. It was exactly the sort of work that she hated, but her mother was incapable of shouldering it. For the rest of that decade, Florence also had the burden of finding someone capable of caring for her mother, who basically needed around-the-clock monitoring. In a letter to her friend, Mary Clarke, Nightingale wrote that attending to her senile mother was harder than anything she had done in the Crimea.

By 1872 Nightingale realized that the nurse training program she had started at St. Thomas's Hospital was not achieving its goals. The new hospital had been built and christened in 1871, but over the years since its inception, Nightingale had come to believe that nurses in training in her namesake program were not getting an adequate education. Strong evidence came in two forms. Nightingale had continued to read the daily journals of the trainees, and she was still issuing her reports on their progress. She was appalled, however, at what she read in the journals. Trainees demonstrated no ability to assess their patients' issues. They were getting little instruction from ward sisters and hospital doctors. Trainees were overworked while trained nurses stood idle.

Nightingale also summoned nurses and students of the program to her home to make reports to her in person. A particularly damning piece of evidence was the report of one of the program's graduates, Rebecca Strong. In her formal written complaint, she stated that she had not been taught anything about anatomy or physiology, and she could not in good conscience recommend the program to anyone.

One figure emerged as the chief culprit of the training program's failure: Dr. R.G. Whitfield. Trainees agreed unanimously that he never taught any classes and never gave any lectures. Beyond that, there were reports that he frequently drank to intoxication, and there was some question of whether his behavior toward female staff could stand up to investigation. Rumors of "impropriety" surrounded him. Whitfield lashed out against these criticisms by condemning the training program itself. Nightingale's standards were simply too high and unrealistic, he averred. In 1872 Nightingale demanded and received Whitfield's resignation from the hospital.

Over the years, the program recovered from its early setbacks. Though it has been through several mergers, the Florence Nightingale School of Nursing and Midwifery is still going strong today under the umbrella of London's Kings College.

In the 1880s, Nightingale continued to lobby on behalf of Indian nationals. In 1883 she saw an opportunity to right injustice in India through the Ilbert Bill. The bill proposed that Indian judges should have the right to try and sentence Europeans who committed criminal acts. This bill had tremendous potential to correct injustice in a country where an Englishman who abused or harassed an Indian national would be tried only by sympathetic countrymen.

Nightingale supported passage of the bill through several channels, both public and private. It was a strategy that had, after all, worked well for her in the past. Privately, she sent letters to key politicians, arguing for the bill. Publicly, she wrote articles. Her paper "The Dumb Shall Speak, and the Deaf Shall Hear" indicted the use of "zemindars" in the process of tax collection. Britain had commissioned zemindars to extract taxes from poor and landless Indians, but the zemindars were extorting additional sums from their victims, and the fear of riots was imminent. Her next article, "Our Indian Stewardship," published in *Nineteenth Century*, specifically argued for the Ilbert Bill. The bill was passed the next year.

1887 brought another reform that Nightingale had hoped for twenty-two years earlier, when she began the battle for Indian reform: for the first time, female nurses were engaged to serve in British military hospitals at Umballa and Rawalpindi in India. The thirty-six nurses were hand-picked by the Surgeon General with Nightingale's input.

By the mid-1880s, Nightingale had publicly declared her support for a free India. Together with a couple of sympathetic allies, she called for the creation of a British Committee of the Indian National Congress. The Indian National Congress was the organization that had been campaigning for nationals' rights and independence for many years. The British Committee, established in 1889, was created to support that cause from within the United Kingdom. As the movement to free India gained traction, Nightingale supported it by hosting meetings and interviews with Indian delegates in her South Street home.

Nightingale was still anxious to improve overall health in India as well as advance independence. In 1894, at the age of seventy-four, she wrote a paper titled "Village Sanitation in India," which was presented at a scientific conference in Hungary. In 1896 she published "Health Missionaries For Rural India."

Last Years

In her mid-seventies, Florence Nightingale embraced a new scientific theory that changed the face of medicine. Prompted by Louis Pasteur's experiments in microbiology, Joseph Lister's advocacy of antiseptic surgery, and the writings of Robert Koch, Nightingale was brought over to the germ theory of disease transmission. It must be noted that Nightingale's insistence on environmental cleanliness and immediate disposal of human waste worked to stop contagion from spreading, regardless of the theory behind those actions. Nightingale's lingering reluctance to embrace germs as the culprit in disease transmission had been twofold. Firstly, she was worried that wholesale acceptance of the germ theory could take emphasis off of the patient. Caregivers would be so anxious to protect themselves from contagion that they might not administer the proper care to the sick. In the nineteenth century, there was every reason to be afraid of your patients. Many nurses died as a direct result of contracting patient diseases, especially typhoid. Even one nurse in Nightingale's School of Nursing succumbed to typhoid in the program's infancy. Secondly, Nightingale had reservations about quarantining patients—which would obviously be indicated if the germ theory were proved true.

Nevertheless, by 1894 the evidence for germ theory was too overwhelming to be ignored. At least it could not be ignored by a mind as logical and scientific as that of Florence Nightingale. In her late seventies, she wrote an entry for *A Dictionary of Medicine* that broke down the implications of germ theory for nurses. Nurses, she wrote, must understand the mechanism of contagion and the function of antiseptic. She recommended the use of specific antiseptic agents such as carbolic acid and chlorinated soda. Nurses must be aware that even the cuff of a uniform could carry contagion, she warned.

When she was eighty-one, the world went dim for Florence Nightingale as it had for her mother. She had fought against encroaching blindness for years, but in 1901 it was no longer possible for her to read her own correspondence. During her last years, she was cared for full-time by May Thorne, a woman doctor. Nightingale lived to be ninety and retained her faculties for most of the years up to her death—suffering confusion only at the end, when she sometimes spoke to beloved family members and friends who had passed on.

Two years before her death, Nightingale was still sharp enough to question the value of the honors heaped upon her by a loving British public. The City of London honored Nightingale with the

"Freedom of the City of London." She was the second woman in history to receive that award. In conjunction with the award, the city proposed to present Nightingale with a gold box that would be commissioned for the occasion. Nightingale learned of this proposal and asked that the one hundred guineas it would cost to make the box be donated, instead, to her old stomping ground, the Institution for the Care of Sick Gentlewomen on Harley Street. Nightingale's hint was taken, and the money went to Harley Street.

Conclusion

Has there ever been someone who accomplished so much and at the same time thought less of herself? Before she had even turned forty, Florence Nightingale was the darling of the British public, the heroine of the Crimea. She could have sailed home to England and comfortably dined out on her fame for the remainder of her long days.

Instead, she conducted a ruthless post-mortem on every moment of her wartime service and found herself entirely wanting. She did not try to hide her mistakes; instead, she sought to broadcast them so that everyone would understand what happens in unsanitary medical facilities. She could well have slid into self-pity and inertia, yet she spent the next several decades campaigning for reforms.

And her reforms are legion. Much of contemporary hospital design was inspired by Nightingale's vision of pavilioned hospitals with wings. All of the little rituals we practice to stop the spread of disease—hand washing, flushing toilets, clean sheets—can be traced back to the influence of Florence Nightingale. Every time the Centers for Disease Control conduct an analysis of how a disease is spreading, too, they use a methodology that was developed, in part, by Florence

Nightingale. Even the infrastructure of contemporary welfare programs is also heavily influenced by Nightingale.

One hundred and fifty years ago, the respect we now have for nurses and the intense training that nurses must undergo was nothing but a seed in Florence Nightingale's imagination. If we believe that nurses are some of the most respectable and hardworking people in our community, we owe that belief to Florence Nightingale. But she never took the credit. As an old woman of seventy-seven, she deflected all her accomplishments onto God with the words, "How inefficient I was in the Crimea! Yet He has raised up Trained Nursing from it!

Please enjoy the first two chapters of Pope Francis: Pastor of Mercy, written by Michael J. Ruszala, as available from Wyatt North Publishing.

Pope Francis: Pastor of Mercy
Chapter 1

There is something about Pope Francis that captivates and delights people, even people who hardly know anything about him. He was elected in only two days of the conclave, yet many who tried their hand at speculating on who the next pope might be barely included him on their lists. The evening of Wednesday, March 13, 2013, the traditional white smoke poured out from the chimney of the Sistine Chapel and spread throughout the world by way of television, Internet, radio, and social media, signaling the beginning of a new papacy.

As the light of day waned from the Eternal City, some 150,000 people gathered watching intently for any movement behind the curtained door to the loggia of St. Peter's. A little after 8:00 p.m., the doors swung open and Cardinal Tauran emerged to pronounce the traditional and joyous Latin formula to introduce the new Bishop of Rome: "Annuncio vobis gaudium magnum; habemus papam!" ("I announce to you a great joy: we have a pope!") He then announced the new Holy Father's identity: "Cardinalem Bergoglio..."

The name Bergoglio, stirred up confusion among most of the faithful who flooded the square that were even more clueless than the television announcers were, who scrambled to figure out who exactly the new pope was. Pausing briefly, Cardinal

Tauran continued by announcing the name of the new pope: "...qui sibi nomen imposuit Franciscum" ("who takes for himself the name Francis"). Whoever this man may be, his name choice resonated with all, and the crowd erupted with jubilant cheers. A few moments passed before the television announcers and their support teams informed their global audiences that the man who was about to walk onto the loggia dressed in white was Cardinal Jorge Mario Bergoglio, age 76, of Buenos Aires, Argentina.

To add to the bewilderment and kindling curiosity, when the new pope stepped out to the thunderous applause of the crowd in St. Peter's Square, he did not give the expected papal gesture of outstretched arms. Instead, he gave only a simple and modest wave. Also, before giving his first apostolic blessing, he bowed asking the faithful, from the least to the greatest, to silently pray for him. These acts were only the beginning of many more words and gestures, such as taking a seat on the bus with the cardinals, refusing a popemobile with bulletproof glass, and paying his own hotel bill after his election, that would raise eyebrows among some familiar with papal customs and delight the masses.

Is he making a pointed critique of previous pontificates? Is he simply posturing a persona to the world at large to make a point? The study of the life of Jorge Mario Bergoglio gives a clear answer, and the answer is no. This is simply who he is as a man and as a priest. The example of his thought- provoking gestures flows from his character, his life experiences, his religious vocation, and his spirituality. This book uncovers the life of the 266th Bishop of Rome, Jorge Mario Bergoglio, also known as Father Jorge, a name he preferred even while he was an archbishop and cardinal.

What exactly do people find so attractive about Pope Francis? Aldo Cagnoli, a layman who developed a friendship with the Pope when he was serving as a cardinal, shares the following: "The greatness of the man, in my humble opinion lies not in building walls or seeking refuge behind his wisdom and office, but rather in dealing with everyone judiciously, respectfully, and with humility, being willing to learn at any moment of life; that is what Father Bergoglio means to me" (as quoted in Ch. 12 of Pope Francis: Conversations with Jorge Bergoglio, previously published as El Jesuita [The Jesuit]).

At World Youth Day 2013, in Rio de Janeiro, Brazil, three million young people came out to celebrate their faith with Pope

Francis. Doug Barry, from EWTN's Life on the Rock, interviewed youth at the event on what features stood out to them about Pope Francis. The young people seemed most touched by his authenticity. One young woman from St. Louis said, "He really knows his audience. He doesn't just say things to say things... And he is really sincere and genuine in all that he does." A friend agreed: "He was looking out into the crowd and it felt like he was looking at each one of us...." A young man from Canada weighed in: "You can actually relate to [him]... for example, last night he was talking about the World Cup and athletes." A young woman added, "I feel he means what he says... he practices what he preaches... he states that he's there for the poor and he actually means it."

The Holy Spirit guided the College of Cardinals in its election of Pope Francis to meet the needs of the Church following the historic resignation of Pope Benedict XVI due to old age. Representing the growth and demographic shift in the Church throughout the world and especially in the Southern Hemisphere, Pope Francis is the first non-European pope in almost 1,300 years. He is also the first Jesuit pope. Pope Francis comes with a different background and set of experiences. Both as archbishop and as pope, his flock knows him for his humility, ascetic frugality in solidarity with the poor, and closeness. He was born in Buenos Aires to a family of Italian immigrants, earned a diploma in chemistry, and followed a priestly vocation in the Jesuit order after an experience of God's mercy while receiving the sacrament of Reconciliation. Even though he is known for his smile and humor, the world also recognizes Pope Francis as a stern figure that stands against the evils of the world and challenges powerful government officials, when necessary.

The Church he leads is one that has been burdened in the West by the aftermath of sex abuse scandals and increased secularism. It is also a Church that is experiencing shifting in numbers out of the West and is being challenged with religious persecution in the Middle East, Asia, and Africa. The Vatican that Pope Francis has inherited is plagued by cronyism and scandal. This Holy Father knows, however, that his job is not merely about numbers, politics, or even success. He steers clear of pessimism knowing that he is the head of Christ's Body on earth and works with Christ's grace. This is the man God has chosen in these times to lead his flock.

Chapter 2: Early Life in Argentina

Jorge Mario Bergoglio was born on December 17, 1936, in the Flores district of Buenos Aires. The district was a countryside locale outside the main city during the nineteenth century and many rich people in its early days called this place home. By the time Jorge was born, Flores was incorporated into the city of Buenos Aires and became a middle class neighborhood. Flores is also the home of the beautiful Romantic-styled Basilica of San José de Flores, built in 1831, with its dome over the altar, spire over the entrance, and columns at its facade. It was the Bergoglios' parish church and had much significance in Jorge's life.

Jorge's father's family had arrived in Argentina in 1929, immigrating from Piedimonte in northern Italy. They were not the only ones immigrating to the country. In the late nineteenth century, Argentina became industrialized and the government promoted immigration from Europe. During that time, the land prospered and Buenos Aires earned the moniker "Paris of the South." In the late nineteenth and early twentieth centuries waves of immigrants from Italy, Spain, and other European countries came off ships in the port of Buenos Aires. Three of Jorge's great uncles were the first in the family to immigrate to Argentina in 1922 searching for better employment opportunities after World War I. They established a paving company in Buenos Aires and built a four-story building for their company with the city's first elevator. Jorge's father and paternal grandparents followed the brothers in order to keep the family together and to escape Mussolini's fascist regime in Italy. Jorge's father and grandfather also helped with the business for a time. His father, Mario, who had been an accountant for a rail company in Italy, provided similar services for the family business (Cardinal Bergoglio recalls more on the story of his family's immigration and his early life in Ch. 1 of Conversations with Jorge Bergoglio).

Providentially, the Bergoglios were long delayed in liquidating their assets in Italy; this forced them to miss the ship they planned to sail on, the doomed Pricipessa Mafalda, which sank off the northern coast of Brazil before reaching Buenos Aires. The family took the Giulio Cesare instead and arrived safely in Argentina with Jorge's Grandma Rosa. Grandma Rosa wore a fur coat stuffed with the money the family brought with them from Italy. Economic hard times eventually hit Argentina in 1932 and the family's paving business went under, but the Bergoglio brothers began anew.

Jorge's father, Mario, met his mother Regina at Mass in 1934. Regina was born in Argentina, but her parents were also Italian immigrants. Mario and Regina married the following year after meeting. Jorge, the eldest of their five children, was born in 1936. Jorge fondly recalls his mother gathering the children around the radio on Sunday afternoons to listen to opera and explain the story. A true porteño, as the inhabitants of the port city of Buenos Aires are called, Jorge liked to play soccer, listen to Latin music, and dance the tango. Jorge's paternal grandparents lived around the corner from his home. He greatly admired his Grandma Rosa, and keeps her written prayer for her grandchildren with him until this day. Jorge recalls that while his grandparents kept their personal conversations in Piedmontese, Mario chose mostly to speak Spanish, preferring to look forward rather than back. Still, Jorge grew up speaking both Italian and Spanish.

Upon entering secondary school at the age of thirteen, his father insisted that Jorge begin work even though the family, in their modest lifestyle, was not particularly in need of extra income. Mario Bergoglio wanted to teach the boy the value of work and found several jobs for him during his adolescent years. Jorge worked in a hosiery factory for several years as a cleaner and at a desk. When he entered technical school to study food chemistry, Jorge found a job working in a laboratory. He worked under a woman who always challenged him to do his work thoroughly. He remembers her, though, with both fondness and sorrow. Years later, she was kidnapped and murdered along with members of her family because of her political views during the Dirty War, a conflict in the 1970's and 80's between the military dictatorship and guerrilla fighters in which thousands of Argentineans disappeared.

Initially unhappy with his father's decision to make him work, Jorge recalls later in his life that work was a valuable formative experience for him that taught him responsibility, realism, and how the world operated. He learned that a person's self worth often comes from their work, which led him to become committed later in life to promote a just culture of work rather than simply encouraging charity or entitlement. He believes that people need meaningful work in order to thrive. During his boyhood through his priestly ministry, he experienced the gulf in Argentina between the poor and the well off, which left the poor having few opportunities for gainful employment.

At the age of twenty-one, Jorge became dangerously ill. He was diagnosed with severe pneumonia and cysts. Part of his upper right lung was removed, and each day Jorge endured the pain and discomfort of saline fluid pumped through his chest to clear his system. Jorge remembers that the only person that was able to comfort him during this time was a religious sister who had catechized him from childhood, Sister Dolores. She exposed him to the true meaning of suffering with this simple statement: "You are imitating Christ." This stuck with him, and his sufferings during that time served as a crucible for his character, teaching him how to distinguish what is important in life from what is not. He was being prepared for what God was calling him to do in life, his vocation.

CPSIA information can be obtained
at www.ICGtesting.com
Printed in the USA
BVOW06s2146270917
496143BV00013B/160/P